HEAVEN
THE
UNDISCOVERED
COUNTRY

HEAVEN

THE
UNDISCOVERED
COUNTRY

Robert C. Broderick

Our Sunday Visitor Publishing Division
Our Sunday Visitor, Inc.
Huntington, IN 46750

Copyright © 1990 by
Our Sunday Visitor Publishing Division
Our Sunday Visitor, Inc.
ALL RIGHTS RESERVED

ISBN: 0-87973-446-9
LCCCN: 90-60639

PRINTED IN THE UNITED STATES OF AMERICA

Cover design by James E. McIlrath

But that the dread of something after death,
The undiscovered country from whose bourn
No traveler returns, puzzles the will,
And makes us rather bear those ills we have
Than fly to others that we know not of.
— W. Shakespeare: *Hamlet III*, 1, 56

Introduction

The subject of this book is heaven. It is a subject which enjoys a special distinction. It compares to nothing else that we know. It is beyond our present experience, yet it commands our attention, not as a constant value of living, but as the ultimate in the comparison of all values. It brings to mind all kinds of feelings and emotions about living and dying, and about millions of different encounters with people and places, with fears and joys.

In man's thinking there are two ways of looking at heaven. The first is through the Christian teachings of hope and belief. This is where we meet the revealed doctrine, the testimony of Christ's coming, His message, His death and resurrection. This is also the learning and acceptance through faith of the way one can ascend to heaven, after being shown the way (Jn. 3:13). This is the final triumph for the Christian, the participation in the fullness of life and in the promised glory of everlasting life with the divine Son of God (Jn. 17:24). In Christian faith-understanding heaven is the final place or state of sharing the glory of God the Father, where the potential of everyone's being will be complete in accord with the will of the Creator. For the Christian heaven is the transformation of all worldly values into the truth of truths. It is the dawn beyond all dawnings when the familiar goodness of promise and reward becomes a reality.

"Then I saw a new heaven and a new earth. The former heaven and the former earth had passed away, and the sea was no more... I heard a loud voice from the throne saying, 'Behold, God's dwelling is with the human race. He will dwell with them and they will be his people and God himself will always be with them [as their God]. He will wipe every tear from their eyes, and there shall be no more death or mourning, wailing or pain, [for] the old order has passed away' " (Rv. 21:1-4).

And, "Nothing accursed will be found there anymore. The throne of God and of the Lamb will be in it, and his servants will worship him. They will look upon his face, his name will be on their foreheads. Night will be no more, nor will they need light from lamp or sun, for the Lord God shall give them light, and they shall reign forever and ever" (Rv. 22:3-5).

This is in stark contrast to the current human failing which wrongly declares there is no heaven, no meaning, no intelligible universe because it has no purpose, because it is godless. One would have to be a fool to make such a claim, surely no intelligent, reasonable person would claim such. A meaningless universe is just that — meaningless and not worth thinking about. Hence, unthinking persons go about in what Leo Strauss called the joyless quest for joy.

The other way of looking at heaven is with the natural, wondrous speculation and studied conjecture that leads us to say, "This must be true because we know and observe." All rational thinking must begin with this world, the natural world, yes, the world of God. It is a reasonable desire that we should want to satisfy our curiosity — that we should want to pick something up and examine it while at the same time speculate or guess about this heaven which so fascinates us. In this heaven we see happiness and joy, nature and supernature, living and life forever.

It is this natural speculation, this concern with joy that we will examine. We do this not because we spurn the teachings of faith and their enlightenment, but because we know in our minds that there are facts which our reason can look at and be consoled by simply because we do look and raise questions in hope. Heaven has the unusual renown of being that about which we know so little, about which our knowledge limps and our guesses founder, and so is hidden in fear, mystery, and the unknown. Therefore, we want to look at heaven as closely as we can in the light of what we do know. To take such a close look we do not consider ourselves foolhardy, but reasonably curious and, yes, even eager to learn what little we can.

The very thought of heaven should be joyous — like looking forward to the start of a very pleasant journey. It is a subject which, if we give up taboos and put aside rigid theologies, may become a warm conjecture and a most fascinating thought to draw us onward. Why don't we think more about heaven? Mainly because of the subjective and the ever present consciousness of the prelude to heaven which is death, about which our instincts fill us with trembling even though we know that death is only the gateway to eternity. But the fact of death should not prevent our thinking about heaven. On the contrary, it should, simply because it is the precondition, urge us to think seriously about death as the beginning, and also to consider more joyfully what is to follow. To this end we must turn our minds to an exploration, to our own encounter with the reasonableness, the thought, the joy which can come only from having a better understanding of this most enticing subject, our own heaven — our undiscovered country.

Today we have heard much about the "near death" experiences of some people. Some of these people were examined and reported on by Doctors Elizabeth Kubler-Ross and Raymond A. Moody, Jr. Their accounts are clinical and chance recordings of what people experienced as they were thought to be dying. Some felt "out of the body" encounters, so to speak, conscious observations of sensitive people who were near to the landscape of the undiscovered country. When they recovered full bodily existence they were profoundly moved and able to recall in some detail their first impressions of the transition from physical life to spiritual life. Undoubtedly there are many others not recorded who have had similar experiences. The two doctors also examined the Bible, the works of Plato, the writings of Emmanuel Swedenborg, and *The Tibetan Book of The Dead*. None of these works "squared" with the modern accounts, but then they also did not offer any direct, knowledgeable insights which would contraindicate that such experiences can be genuine.

We too have looked into some of these writings, in addition to the legends and lore of native American Indians and the folklore of other peoples. We make no definitive choice of an explicit description of what heaven may or may not be. For the most part, however, we will consider the one prime source of Christians everywhere, as well as Moslems and Jews, namely the Bible. We do not do this to make faith stand as the only alternative to reason, but rather to introduce the words of revelation insofar as we understand them. For it is there that we read what little is recorded about the alluring subject of heaven. No other writing teaches so much with the ring of authority. In the Bible there is no definite description, no pictured thought, no graphic delineation of actual experiences. Instead the accounts are at best vague and metaphorical, but they lead the mind to an outward, beyond nature state which, when joined with faith and a hopeful disposition, lead us deep into the real joy of the mystery. We must be content with this for the present. We can add only what can be reasonably speculated about heaven, what we can conjecture in reason if not through informed imagination. Someone once said "death is not a matter of going into darkness — it is a turning down of the lamp, for the dawn is coming."

Heaven, we may say, is not merely a poetic fancy. Nor is it a total unknown, wrapped in a blanket of myth and mystery, hidden under a bushel, and existing only in a "cloud of unknowing." Rather heaven is a joyous condition, a merry place of glory about which we really know more than we are aware, garnered from our reading of literature. It is a subject about which, when we stop to think, we do have some rather definite ideas. But it is full of the intrigue of the unknown, beautiful vistas toward which we look with quiet speculation — for every person of reason it is the great adventuresome place to which each of us looks with a subtle, longing anticipation. The majority of people believe that heaven is their eventual destination. While a few may think of it as a nothing-place, there is a surprisingly large number of those who know their place in heaven as well as they know their pews in church.

Aware of this wide interest in heaven, even if not consciously admitted, we address ourselves to the subject with an openness of mind, a probing, searching, thinking attitude. It is a curious fact that no one knows anything absolutely certain about heaven, even though most believe they are headed "that-a-way" no matter what. At least that is what they claim. As "Life" magazine once declared editorially, "The Christian hope is nothing less than the hope of heaven, and this hope is central to Christian faith." Ask them what they hope for and the answer is strong and clear, "Heaven is ours, alleluia!"

Even so, people who don't know what to do on a Saturday afternoon let alone a Sunday morning, sometimes wonder and worry about what they will be doing in the hereafter. This is where this book comes in. It is not intended to give them an answer, point the way, or fill in the outlines of faith. Rather we hope to provide a clear look at the reality of our certain future. We are going to take a reasonable look at heaven and see just how it will fit us for size and other details. We know what we would like, but what are we going to get? Granted, this, of course, is a large order. Heywood Broun has said: "Very few writers have been able to present an acceptable abode for the blessed. Any fool can do hell." We are not going to write about hell now — or even think about it as an alternative. Admittedly, our task would be easier if God had followed the suggestion of one writer that "there should be windows in heaven and skylights in hell."

Actually, it shouldn't be too difficult to make a good, rounded appraisal of heaven. That is, if we actually want to think about it instead of running away from the idea until it is too late. Our look at heaven is going to be a straightforward one, reasonable, free of all the folderol and silly guessing that we could indulge in without fear of any contradiction. We put the proposition quite simply: since there is a God, there is a heaven. Wrestle with the first half of that statement in any way you wish, in the light of faith and love and hope, while we take a "start-of-an-adventure" look at the latter half. As with most adventures, ours will be merry rather than morbid. Perhaps we all will be caught up in heaven's brilliance. Maybe we will be blinded and dazzled by the splendor of what we learn, taught by its greatness of joy to be forever dissatisfied with the smallness and meanness of everyday living.

We want our consideration to be happy and not stodgy, not filled with exhortations about all the naughty things that are supposed to be like a time-lock on heaven and all the goody-goody things that are said to be the combination to the lock. Our reasonable look at heaven is intended to offer a happy preview, an insight. It should be similar to getting ready for a trip, feeling the joy of anticipation more than getting bogged down with the details of the journey. It may even help our lifelong planning for the promised joys.

Every strategy for gaining goals, achieving ambitions, begins with a dream. Let these words that follow be a planned strategy, a beginning for attaining our ultimate goal which should be heaven.

I

To heaven's high city I direct my journey,
Whose spangled suburbs entertain my eye.
— F. Quarles, *Emblems*, Bk. V

While we are looking forward and enjoying ourselves, we can consider what we do and don't know about heaven. First, we believe that it exists. Oh, not all of us believe this in the same way. Some, like Mohammedans, think of it as a place of special delight where the harem is going to be what their imagination dreams a harem should be other than the headache it is in actuality. Others, like ancestor worshippers, think of heaven as a place peopled with nothing but relatives (and where some people might wish to be orphans). A few, who look forward to reincarnation as a progressive step toward perfection, think it would be fine to be born repeatedly anew in some form, completely forgetting that this means to be born repeatedly to die. By using our powers of reason, we shall see that this is utterly ridiculous because: to be reborn later, after being a human being, in the form of a cat or bird is a denial of God as Creator of humans as the greatest and most dignified and free of all His creations. The hallmark of man is the ability to think, and thinking ultimately leads to a consideration of heaven as the one, ultimate destination.

There are certain people, less knowing than we, who say, "That's all right for the soul, but when my body, the old Adam, is tucked neatly away, that's the end." These are usually the followers of the "eat, drink, and be merry" formula of living — Epicureans who seize the fleeting good and don't look forward to the future. Give them a good lusty fistful of life and they think they'll be satisfied for now and forever, ready "to give up the ghost" and leave this life with as pleasant a "burp" as they can manage. Some too, even less gifted, feel that when they have shucked off the body, it will return from what they call "super space," a sort of dimensionless waiting-room, and be born again as an animal or another person. As far as heaven is concerned, they do not care to give it a serious thought. How ridiculous for anyone to think that God, who made each man and woman unique, could be limited by forcing His creations into lesser creatures — unless one wants to think that humans are inferior to the beasts. And as for being another person at some future time, the law of contradiction ever stands in the way of that idea.

With many people it is a waste of time to argue, since we know heaven is simply not a hangover from a lifelong binge. We are seriously concerned with heaven, with what we can speculate about it, as well as what we hope for in the promised resurrection of the body. Just when this resurrection of all bodies will take place we don't know. The pseudomystics making their predictions don't know either. Will it be soon after all humans have died? Who knows any more than those who profess to know when the world will end — like the modern prophets, the latest being Magdalene Porzat, who said: "In the year when Easter occurs on the feast of St. Mark (April 25), Pentecost on the feast of St. Anthony (June 13), and Corpus Christi occurs on the feast of St. John the Baptist (June 24), then the whole world will cry: Woe! Woe! Woe!" (1943 was one such year, and not a very good one we'll admit. The next year these events will coincide will be 2038.) All this sounds too much like the children's game: "I know something you don't know." It's a fact that no living person really knows — period!

In fact, the date of resurrection of all peoples has been and always will be the greatest of secrets. Legend has it that Gabriel, the Archangel, is waiting in the wings with his hand on the trumpet ready to sound the call to assembly. But this is only symbol and myth. We learn from the Bible that Christ spoke of the general resurrection as the final event on the agenda of activities for the last day. It will come about only when time ends — and that will be soon enough.

There are more modern concepts, as that of Chardin, wherein man evolves into a oneness of being, perfected and extended in time to the infinite — this idea is based upon the older idea of Sophia, the world-soul which absorbs all, making a universal deism. But the truer belief we have is that heaven is not a substantial transformation into God but the evolution of man to supernatural happiness. It is where God is — and this is difficult for us to comprehend because we think in human terms and in that context we cannot understand that God is "spirit" and exists independent of anything smaller, larger, firmer, softer, or having any boundaries or other limitations. Hence God cannot and does not have a "home" or keep an office somewhere. We will return to this later.

The fact emerges, even for hard-core atheists, there has always existed in the world, perhaps not revealed or deduced by reason, a religious inwardness which is a desire, a need to believe in a God, a supreme being. This is joined with a desire to believe; a desire to adore with love; a desire to humiliate oneself in total, timeless veneration; a desire to live, to elevate oneself by approaching an observed but seemingly inaccessible ideal. All our liturgy, modes of worship, building of altars, singing and incantations are the products of men expressing this desire. God and man are on a journey toward each other. God has arrived, but we have not. God is concerned with all things and all persons and all men and women are drawn to Him because of this shared desire and the need to attain the reward, the fullness of love.

We know that heaven is something to be attained, something that will satisfy our every aspiration. A mechanic looking at a fine engine can tell you, without running it, how well it will perform. And a man can look at himself and realize that he has an infinite capacity for happiness which everything on earth could not satisfy. So he reasons that there must be a heaven since he knows that God could not be so cruel as to give man infinite desire and then not provide infinite happiness, just as no man would create an engine and never run it. Or to put it another way: we know that here on earth we are but the blossom, yet in heaven we will be the fruit. This fruit is the fullness of the promise which was in the bud and in the blossom and even in the dying of the blossom.

Heaven has been celebrated in literature and song, in drama and folklore. A few writers not only have denied it but also have ridiculed it. Yet for decades heaven has been used consistently as the comparative by which every joy and fulfillment is measured. In human love it has been used to portray the utmost in happiness — "It would be heavenly to be with you!"

Heaven is spoken of in the Bible some 200 times directly or indirectly, but mostly in metaphor. Nowhere is it described in detail. It is "Paradise," the "New Jerusalem," the "House of many mansions." In figure it is "spacious," but this must be accepted as only a metaphorical description. St. John writes: "And in the Spirit he carried me away to a great, high mountain, and showed me the holy city Jerusalem coming down out of heaven from God, having the glory of God, its radiance like a most rare jewel, like a jasper, clear as crystal. It had a great, high wall, with twelve gates, and at the gates twelve angels, and on the gates the names of the twelve tribes of the sons of Israel were inscribed; on the east three gates, on the north three gates, on the south three gates, and on the west three gates. And the wall of the city had twelve foundations, and on them the twelve names of the twelve apostles of the Lamb.

"And he who talked to me had a measuring rod of gold to measure the city and its gates and walls. The city lies foursquare, its length the same as its breadth; and he measured the city with his rod, twelve thousand stadia; its length and breadth and height are equal. He also measured its wall, a hundred and forty-four cubits by a man's measure, that is, an angel's. The wall was built of jasper, while the city was pure gold, clear as glass. The foundations of the wall of the city were adorned with every jewel; the first was jasper, the second sapphire, the third agate, the fourth emerald, the fifth onyx, the sixth carnelian, the seventh chrysolite, the eighth beryl, the ninth topaz, the tenth chrysoprase, the eleventh jacinth, the twelfth amethyst, and the twelve gates were twelve pearls, each of the gates made of a single pearl, and the street of the city was pure gold, transparent as glass" (Rev. 21:10-21 — Revised Standard Version, Thomas Nelson & Sons, Ltd.).

Such a biblical description, which is different from another found in chapters forty to forty-eight of Ezekiel, is limited by the writer's own means of expression, and by the understanding of those for whom he wrote. It is not a description that with any stretch of the imagination approximates the condition of the heavenly abode, nor does it approach physical beauty according to any standard of present day values. Rather it is a way of saying that in death one era ends and a new one begins — one life closes and a door is opened onto a new life of unimaginable beauty. It tries to supply our imagination with a visual dream and promises that the dream will become a reality and the reality will be the truth.

Also, heaven has been written of in the most magnificent poetry, as in the culminating portion of Dante's *Divine Comedy* where it is hailed as Paradise. Dante exclaims of heaven: "Meseemed I was beholding a smile of the universe; wherefore my intoxication entered both by hearing and by sight. O joy! O gladness unspeakable! O life compact of love and peace! O wealth secure that hath no longing!" (*Par.* Can. 27). Likewise, Milton majestically declared it to be the ultimate in the lost-and-found departments, and life a "long or short permit to heaven." A German proverb promises, "heaven for climate, hell for company." Sidney Smith said his idea of heaven was the everlasting eating of *foie gras* to the sound of trumpets; and the poet Heine said, "In heaven roast geese fly around... everywhere there are bowls of bouillon and champagne." Our own folk songs call it "The Big Rock-Candy Mountain" which describes a hobo's idea of heaven. The poet Christina Rosetti declared, "Heaven is the presence of God"; while Elbert Hubbard wisecracked that heaven was the "Coney Island of the Christian imagination."

Many have enlarged upon their own ideas, added to those of the biblical writers, certain that it is a place of peace, pleasure, eternal happiness, rest, and surcease from the sorrows of our lives, yet filled with unexpected delights as well.

Others seek to console us according to the Bible by declaring heaven to be a place of no moths, no thieves, no rust — and no giving and taking in marriage. These many perambulations of words merely proclaim that heaven is looked upon, both frivolously and seriously, pretty much according to one's taste — and maybe we can refine our taste and our faith. Norman Cousins in his *Celebration of Life* offers this as one of his logical conclusions: "I believe that the expansion of knowledge makes for an expansion of faith, and the widening of the horizons of mind for a widening of belief. My reason nourishes my faith and my faith my reason."

Heaven has been written of and spoken about in terms less majestic and rather more endearing, as in Connolly's *Green Pastures*, the place from which "Oh God!" came to console and bedazzle a storekeeper. It has also suffered some naive and too-human descriptions, almost childish in their approach. We hear about the "pearly gates." We joke about St. Peter standing there as the eternal custodian waiting for the password, sifting out the unworthy, or directing our mode of transportation to a heavenly parking-lot. Stories, anecdotes, and jokes about heaven have humor that is rather pathetic in its absurdity. But these stories and bandied phrases about heaven are often quite doltish, some even arising out of a literal misunderstanding of the idea that spiritually one must be as a child to enter into the kingdom of heaven.

From our human knowledge we know of the one essential condition for entry into heaven: to enter there one must have died. Everyone living now will fulfill this condition — whether the person looks to heaven as a destination or not. But we are not concerned here and now with how to live, how to get to heaven or how to die. The method to be followed for assuring arrival at heaven is for theologians, learned people of religion — and some of these will themselves miss the final mark by untold miles. As for dying, someone has said that even the lowest cads learn how to do this. The modern world seems to be discovering new and bizarre methods of sending children, men, and women winging on their way to their deaths — and oh so many with untimely speed and dispatch. And dying with or without one's boots on is utterly unimportant as a condition, since boots have nothing to do with heaven. The "resting place," the place of entombment, or the number of flowers and wreaths — none of these relates to heaven in the remotest way. The only certain, really conclusively true fact is that everyone now living is going to die.

Still, beyond a certain natural wonderment about heaven and a genuine curiosity about the place of beatitude, we can well afford to look more directly at heaven. After all, no one buys a ticket for a theater when no play is scheduled there. Concerning the hereafter, we can at least muse upon the great goodness we know exists and try to understand why anyone might want to choose hell even if the rumored social life there may include some of the most gifted and daring people.

Heaven is "the great somewhere" about which we can be reasonable. And the more we get into the subject, examine what we know or even don't know about heaven, we may learn that we will find it alluring, interesting, a place where we really want to be. When we reason about heaven we recall Samuel Johnson's words: "He is no wise man that will quit a certainty for an uncertainty." We look more closely, remembering Henry Thoreau, who, when upon his deathbed, was asked by a friend, "Henry, you're so close to the edge, can you see anything on the other side?" And Henry replied, "One world at a time, my friend!" From this world we can look to the next only with anticipation.

We learn quickly that as soon as we limit, describe in human terms, or measure our view of heaven by our meager standards, we frustrate our own effort. The more expansive, the more all-embracing our grasp is, the more we can appreciate what heaven will mean for us. There are others who can tell us, "Here's how!" But we can and will think about our own destiny and say, "Here's where!"

II

This life is but the passage of a day,
This life is but a pang and all is over,
But in the life to come which fades not away
Every love shall abide and every lover.
— Christina Rossetti, *Saints and Angels*

In the Bible, heaven is called by the name "life," not just "life eternal," but the possession of life in its real sense. This is *all* life, a true, total and complete living as only human persons can come to experience it. Here on earth life is incomplete, just as we know that nature is lacking the full perfection of the supernatural.

We must refer to the question of immortality before we proceed. There are a number of reasonable affirmative declarations that we can make. For example, life is good and because our God is a God of the living, not the dead, we are not presumptive in declaring that man, made in His image, is immortal. The eminence of thought itself is revelatory, for no ideas or thinking are valid which arise from irrational or illogical sources — hence truth perceived by human reason goes on to the ultimate conclusion of its own action. Thus we can declare that the principles of truth are the first and preeminent mark of heaven itself and hence, by extension, of life hereafter and immortality.

To get a better hold on this we come back to our inspiration, the Bible, and hear what Job affirms with strong words: "But as for me, I know that my Vindicator lives, and that he will at last stand forth upon the dust; Whom I myself shall see: my own eyes, not another's, shall behold him, and from my flesh I shall see God; my inmost being is consumed with longing" (Jb. 19:25-26). And Isaiah writes with prophetic insight of the preparation for and the joy of final immortality: "Say to those whose hearts are frightened: Be strong, fear not! Here is your God, he comes with vindication; With divine recompense he comes to save you. Then will the eyes of the blind be opened, the ears of the deaf be cleared; Then will the lame leap like a stag, then the tongue of the dumb will sing" (Is. 35:4-6).

There is also the testimony of modern writers who make clear affirmations from their faith or their longing. "The death (of Christ) only became a source of salvation and of life because it was followed by the resurrection" (A. Lemounyer, French theologian). Rabbi Mordecai Simon says the soul is immortal, and that this world is "a vestibule of the hereafter." William Faulkner, in his acceptance speech when receiving the Nobel prize for literature in 1950, spoke to the world: "I believe that man will not merely endure; he will prevail. He is immortal, not because he alone among all creatures has an inexhaustible voice, but because he has a soul, a spirit capable of compassion and sacrifice and endurance." And Kahlil Gibran proclaims reassuringly in *The Prophet* (p. 88): "And what is it to cease breathing, but to free the breath from its restless tides, that it may rise and expand and see God unencumbered? Only when you drink from the river of silence shall you indeed sing. And when you have reached the mountain top, then shall you begin to climb. And when the earth shall claim your limbs, then shall you truly dance." The constant flow of ideas about immortality can be found throughout the history of humankind and also in continuing traditions as life's tapestry unfolds.

Other reasonable aspects of immortality are dominant in modern thought and we look at them briefly in the light of man's own assessment of the personal and spiritual development of human existence.

Each human being is unique, unlike any other, and has a special personhood, hence we are regarding the whole being of the human person. Immortality for the individual is also unique, and has three essential aspects. First, each has a spiritual identity. In other words each person develops his or her particular and special lifestyle and the mold or quality of spirit or soul. Each sins as no other person sins — for guilt is not equal one to another; each repents, improves, reshapes his life as no other person does. This has always been recognized in man's laws and in social or societal life up to this present time.

Second, there is a vital identity. This means that each person's physiological, psychical, emotional, intellectual life is distinctive in quality and degree. We can demonstrate this with the distinctiveness of fingerprints, no two being identical, as well as the diversity of brain substance and bodily function. All of these are hidden in the infinite variety possible to the genetic makeup of individuals, and their potentials, inherited and environmental.

Third, there is atomic identity. Each person in his or her body has an atomic uniqueness. This extends to the chemistry of the body and the cellular makeup of the genes and tissues which are positively different from every other human being ever created or to be created in the future. (Therefore no exact human cloning is possible.)

These three identities make up the unique nature of every individual and are carried over intact to the immortal life of the human personality. We will consider the immortality of the body later in more detail.

This brings us to the basic method of thought in the light of which we examine heaven reasonably, namely, the *law of contradiction*. Put quite simply this law merely states that something or someone cannot *exist* and *not exist* at the same time; that where there is light there cannot also be darkness; where there is wholeness there cannot be anything lacking. In thinking about heaven the contradiction is in reference to the infinite as opposed to the finite — the unlimited as opposed to the limited.

While this law is naturally true and obvious to our common sense, it is fraught with untold dimensions when we apply it to the supernatural. This is where we must begin with God as Creator, and with His providence, for He cares for what He has created. Because what God has created it is impossible for Him to uncreate. This is a truth that is apparent to the Psalmist:

"Yet with you I shall always be; you have hold of my right hand; With your counsel you guide me, and in the end you will receive me in glory. Whom else have I in heaven? And when I am with you, the earth delights me not. Though my flesh and my heart waste away, God is the rock of my heart and my portion forever" (Rom 73:23-26).

To this law of contradiction we must add another simple natural law — that of *consequences*. This is no more than the application of the law of physics which declares that every action demands a reaction, that an object in motion remains in motion until a greater force halts that motion or overcomes the object's mass and momentum. On the human plane we recognize this when we observe that in nature a mother and father care for their children until that care is no longer required.

Also we have a third law — which is the law of *response*. This means that if there is a noise there is the response of hearing it, or if there is beauty there is the response of seeing it, and so on.

In the light of these essential qualities of immortality and the laws of reason, we find that heaven will be an incomparable adventure, exceedingly interesting and ever beyond our expectations. That is why we must look at it as simply as possible.

We tend, in modern living, to become caught up in making a big deal out of what is really quite simple and ordinary. This is particularly true of our language. A simple declarative sentence, such as those admired by Edwin Newman, seems to be the exception rather than the rule. Note for example, this statement: "Existential imperative mutates into the continuum." What that means is simply that "today changes into tomorrow," or even more simply, the *now* becomes the *then*. We shall try to avoid such high-flowing, obscure language in our thought of heaven.

Some theologians, or as some of them prefer to think of themselves "religion scientists," and professors and savants, doctors, lawyers, sociologists, and politicians like to show their ability to gild the precise with a total lack of understanding by the use of obscure words. These fit the description of the learned people given by Samuel Johnson: "They delight to tread upon the brink of meaning." We must remind ourselves that there is no law which says we more ordinary human persons cannot ask, "What are we? What are we doing? And where are we going?" — all in a simple, clear, and thoughtful way as we look at heaven.

III

Short arm needs man to reach to heaven
So ready is heaven to stoop to him.
— F. Thompson, *Grace of the Way*

Possibly the most interesting aspect of heaven is the multitude of things we don't know about it. We know that it is not a place one can find simply by asking directions from the first person one meets. Such a thought would somehow rob heaven of all its delightful mystery about which we like to speculate. As Sir Thomas Browne said, "Were happiness of the next world as closely apprehended as the felicities of this, it were a martyrdom to live." We can certainly agree with Dante who said that his memory has a certain rule which simply says of heaven, "A new life begins."

Heaven has been defined in many ways, almost as many as there are people to think of definitions. The dictionary has been defining the word for some time as "the expanse of space surrounding the earth." This indicates primarily the arch or dome of space above us in which the sun, moon, stars, gnats, and mesons move and which is sometimes called, for want of a better name, "the firmament." Quite obviously this is not the heaven to which we feel we have a prior claim and toward which we progress with the succession of breaths, minutes, hours, days, and years which are ours.

In the light of recent "outer space" explorations, we have learned that there is a considerable area which, by the above definition, would be considered heaven. And there is no evidence showing any formed boundaries or otherwise delineated space where one might find heaven located. All we do know is that heaven exists and that it is unlimited. We think of it as the abode of God, saints, and angels and as durably infinite. We know heaven to be a mode of existence different from anything we have experienced or considered heretofore. Robert Marchant writing in the *Bulletin of the C.S. Lewis*

Society states: "And this is one of the promises of God, that as He is, so are we. And in our death, resurrection and ascension, space, time, matter and the senses are to be weeded, dug, and sown for a new crop; reformed but not replaced."

The ancient Greeks, wily fellows when it came to putting a label on everything, considered heaven a series of concentric spheres about the earth. They disagreed as to the number, declaring from seven to eleven of these spheres and mixing them with the orbits of the planets and the sun, which latter they thought was moving around the earth. Later they became more definite when they were looking for a place for their gods and came up with the legend of Mount Olympus which they imagined as peopled with all types of well behaved deities who only occasionally had human lapses, frailties, and emotions.

The poet Dante, out to look for a particular place to which he could journey in his poetic phantasy, borrowed from the Greeks and other pagans and described his "Paradise" as a series of nine "heavens or spheres beneath the empyrean." (Note how many people think of heaven as a place *above* the earth, a place which one looks up to or arises to.)

The dictionary has also called heaven "the dwelling place of the Deity." This again is a lame borrowing from the pagans and is much too confining. Better to say it is that state of existence where God's love is most known and experienced. Webster's further expanded the definition to "the celestial abode of bliss" and "the place and state of the living dead." This brought the definition more into keeping with both traditional ideas and modern confusion. It gave heaven some connection with the American Indian's "happy hunting ground," where every arrow could find a ready target. It also permitted that heaven be likened to "Valhalla," the place where the souls of heroes were said to feast and traffic through five hundred and forty gates, going to battle and returning. It even brought heaven into comparison with "Nirvana," the painless perpetual life of oriental religion.

All the many definitions of heaven limp most pitiably, but only because we have not paused to think deeply about heaven, and we find it difficult to get away from human comparisons. John Donne in his twenty-third sermon states: "He that asks me what heaven is, means not to hear me, but to silence me; he knows I cannot tell him: when I meet him there, I shall be able to tell him; and then he will be able to tell me; yet then we shall be able to tell one another this, that we enjoy heaven, but the tongues of glorified saints, shall not be able to express what that heaven is...," as we shall discover in our reasoning about heaven.

Which brings us back to the Bible and a more enlightened aspect of heaven. St. Paul speaks of heaven as "the city of the living God" and the place where the spirits of just men are made perfect (Heb. 12:22-25). But this is not to say heaven is a specific place — but rather that it is a state of existence about which we do not know now.

Suffice it to say that two facts become immediately clear: that heaven is the immanence of God Himself — the "everywhereness" of God; that it is a place of glory. Even now we know we are progressing from one degree of glory to the next. Here "glory" means that which of itself is worthwhile in a person or thing. The progression through a state of growth from year to year is the increment of glory, as is also the growth from accomplishment and so on. This is reflected in the idea of worshipping God. The liturgy, as a here and now participation in the worship of God, has its beginning on earth, and in this sense is an anticipation of the climactic liturgy when all will give final and everlasting praise to God. As Solomon says in the Book of Wisdom, "And thus were the paths of those on earth made straight, and men learned what was your pleasure, and were saved by Wisdom" (Wis. 9:18). And St. Augustine says: "God is the goal of our desires. He is the one whom we shall see without end, whom we shall love without weariness, whom we shall glorify forever without fatigue."

When looked at closely, heaven is not only difficult to define, but it becomes more intriguing. In all the above and other definitions, however, we can detect a certain relationship, with a borrowing or expanding which leads eventually to vagueness unless there is interpretation or some reasonable speculation. One idea, it appears, is surely common to all, namely, that heaven is *up*. One has to look up to heaven; one must raise his eyes; one must strive upward to attain heaven; one must soar aloft to get to heaven.

Not so, we say. This idea is the first misconception from which we must free ourselves before we can reach an enlightened concept of heaven. To say that heaven is above us is all right for poetry, for

Billy Graham when he points his finger to the stars, and for all the fanciful or exhortatory appeals for us to rise to loftier heights. But logically, in human reason, we know that any thing or place that is above us must be supported on some foundation or at least have a suspending force. It must have limits if it is above — or below or beside or outside of something else.

This we can say positively is not true of heaven. Why? First because heaven is infinite, without limit. Second, any physical scientist or engineer can tell you that there is no such thing as absolute zero but only an infinite division of something. From this we can reason: heaven could not be up because whatever is up is there in relation to something else, as your hand is up in relation to the desk or table you hold it above. Now if heaven were up in relation to the earth, it would be relative to the earth, earthbound, so to speak. An infinite place thus bound by a finite place would be inferior, smaller or larger, but it would not be infinite — and if it is not infinite it is limited, and if limited, it cannot be heaven. Therefore, heaven cannot be in any natural or physical place, else it could and would not be infinite — and if you limit heaven you destroy heaven.

Unfortunately, however, we are forced to view heaven from the human side — from our own present limitations. Therefore, our view is bound to be inadequate no matter how we twist or turn our thinking to make it fit the dimensions of our knowledge.

To the fact that heaven is infinite we can add another: no human being ever has returned or will return from heaven to add to what we know now. This is true in spite of extrasensory experiences or stories of ghosts and other strange encounters that we might hear. And the reason for our making such apparently dogmatic statements is that we know we are talking about something superhuman, beyond our experience or experiential possibility, namely the supernatural. We do know that we cannot think about anything that is beyond nature, although we know there are happenings, entire events, beyond our present capabilities of assessment. We have difficulty thinking with any certainty outside the limits of nature. Instead, our thinking must be in the light of the supernatural, which most of us will admit is very intangible considering our limited natural experience. But only in this way can we move beyond our human nature and arrive at an idea of heaven — inadequate and imperfect as this idea may be.

Since this may sound as though we are going into a blind alley of thought, recall for a moment that within all of these limitations we still know more than we thought possible. And we can speculate, within reason and according to what our faith dictates, as much as we wish. With this in mind we can relax a little.

Anyone writing about heaven, reading about it, or just dreaming of it, should be notably joyous. There is a true inner joy which arises from being assured and satisfied that this heaven is what we are striving for, and joy from being reasonably certain that we can realize designated conditions for attaining it. We are less earthbound while thinking of heaven; we are not merely joyous in the manner of a child who has just been given a new pair of shoes and hugs them to himself, thinking the possession of them is heaven obtained. Possessions can bring temporary joy, but they leave us still with emptiness, a feeling of being unfulfilled as persons. We have no grounds to be smug and complacent in knowing that there is a heaven to which we journey. Rather we are encouraged because there is no emptiness, there is no wanting, in heaven.

Quite simply, heaven is a state of being. This can be clarified by taking the words "human being" and striking off the word "human." The portion designated by "human" corresponds to "natural" and it is from this natural standpoint, as we have said, that we view heaven while we are living. It is from the natural plane that most of the misconceptions of heaven arise. We apply to heaven all sorts of mistaken ideas. For instance, a common fallacy is to think of heaven as a place of natural delights — an everlasting "fun and games" existence, where the appetites of the flesh will be satisfied eternally in an orgy of bliss. And this does not even begin to touch upon the mental raptures that we humans suppose are there, according to the desires and fancies we experience on earth.

As long as we remain on the natural plane, it is normal to think of heaven in these terms. After all, that is what we know and experience "in the body." For example, take the idea of a steak in heaven — imagination serves it, done perfectly according to our taste. But continue to think on the natural plane and see what happens: appetite, taste, and savor would have to be perfect also, that is, without the least diminution. And because in heaven we cannot have and not have steak according to the law of contradictions, we face what? We face a condition in which we would have to be eating steak continuously, without ending, without consuming the steak — and that would leave us little else to do. How utterly horrible! For then would come boredom at least, and we know that boredom is an imperfection. Since there can be no imperfections in heaven this would not be heaven but a monotonous, endless orgy of eating. By natural thinking we are simply left trying to fit a square peg into a round hole, something which cannot be done because it is not a "natural" condition. So we come right back to our previous conclusion that we must not attempt to think of heaven in natural, earthbound terms.

IV

By banks where burned awhile the rose
And roved the goldenrod,
I lay through wheeling ages,
Gossiping with God.
— M. Dooher, *Renascence*

The supernatural is the *perfected* natural. The supernatural transcends the natural, bringing the natural to an unimagined perfection. Once the supernatural takes the place of the natural as a state of being, limitations cease and all of the human person becomes perfected. The human then becomes changed and transfigured with two unearthly conditions: the first, is that of "glory." This light of glory is something that transforms us, but it is also something which has its beginning in us even now when we are on earth. In the Bible, St. Paul says: "All of us, gazing with unveiled face on the glory of the Lord, are being transformed into the same image from glory to glory, as from the Lord who is the Spirit" (2 Cor. 3:19). And Dr. Josephine Massyngberde Ford tells us: "Glory means that which is intrinsically worthwhile in a person or thing. Thus heaven will be the climax of our personal growth."

When the Bible speaks of this "light of glory" it does not mean something from outside of us so much as something within which is to be realized as the climax of all we have attempted to gain in our lives. It will be our own unique perfection upon which we are now working. In other words, those natural things which are necessary to the keeping of that word "human" in the term "human being" will be done away with in the supernatural state, made translucent by the "light of glory."

This is not to say that the faculties of the body and soul will no longer exist or function. It means simply that natural faculties, expressive of the human person, will no longer be necessary. We will

31

no longer be "dependent" beings, locked into the human framework and its many limitations. As Dante says, mankind will enjoy the greatest of God's gifts, freedom, with which all are endowed. He also says, "You shall prove how salty is the taste of another man's bread and how hard is the way up and down another man's stairs" (Par. 15:58). This freedom is begun on earth as we participate in the worship and learning about God that goes on all of our lives, for we are free to be uniquely different in degree from every other human person. We differ in the quality of the glory we possess and in the quantity of service which we alone can give in our unique way. As St. Augustine says, in this life we have the freedom to sin, but in heaven we shall have the higher liberty of not being able to sin.

The second transformation in heaven for human persons will be the supernatural state. In this all will be uniquely different because the supernatural brings a new dimension to one's own capacity. You could not see God without this condition, as St. John says, "No one has ever seen God" (Jn. 1:18). It is only in the glorified and supernatural state that one can indeed see God — or possess the exquisite joy of seeing Him face to face or as He is in His being.

In this supernatural state there will also be added those supernatural qualities that will enable a "being" to enjoy heaven as heaven is intended to be enjoyed. It is the utmost of experience of love wherein the rest of the joys of heaven are recognized, and where they are appreciated with satisfaction, rest, and the total glory of our being.

Heaven is a deepening, an intensification of our being. All that we are is made to be the means of enjoying perfect joy in heaven. As human beings composed of body and soul, we are like an acetylene torch which burns a mixture of two gases, and when these two are intensified to the right degree of heat, to the point of brilliant, concentrated flame, it is able to cut through steel. Similarly, in heaven we will be able to cut away the natural and be truly glorified.

For the moment it is necessary to seem to dillydally with this juxtaposition of the natural against the supernatural. Unless we can bring ourselves to distinguish deeply and inwardly the great difference between these two, we won't be able to become free of the human concepts which have led to much of our previous confusion. There is one point to clarify immediately: the supernatural should not be linked with what many think of as the *preternatural* which is sometimes the interference which comes from the *unnatural.* This refers to happenings that are outside of our natural understanding and some of these occurrences may be considered to be diabolical.

Let's swing the tiller around another tack. Heaven will be a unique experience for each unique individual. No one's heaven will be the same as any other person's — because there are no identical individuals in heaven any more than there are identical fingerprints here on earth. Besides, repetition in creation would be a limitation and we know there can be no limitation on God's infinite creativity. No, each one of us will enjoy, participate in, be part of heaven as he or she is, and not as someone else. The reason for this is that heaven means the complete self-realization of the person, the singular perfecting of the individual.

What does this psychological, theological reaching for terms mean? Look at it like this: consider each one of us as a glass. The perfection of a glass is in satisfying its purpose for being, which is as a fully filled container. It is perfected only when it is filled completely. That is the sole purpose of a glass — an empty glass is not fulfilled in its purpose, and a partly filled glass is lacking in satisfying its purpose. In heaven, each one of us will be filled or perfected — made to be what each was intended to be in the wholeness of his or her being. We won't be given short measure like a half cup of coffee, nor will we be overflowing like a size six foot in a four triple-A shoe. Each one will be filled completely, perfectly — and *no two will be alike.* This means that no two persons will enjoy heaven in exactly the same manner or to the same degree. It also follows that even were one to return from heaven to describe it, he would be able to describe it only "subjectively," that is, only in the distinctive manner in which he experiences heaven in his total being.

A challenging question immediately arises. How do we know this — this business about the varying glasses and the perfecting process? We know it, remember, from our recent attempt at supernatural thinking; but we also know it from our reason. We know that each created thing or person is only complete when it is perfected or fulfilled, when it reaches the end or purpose for which it was created. We also know about this "personal" way of enjoying heaven, since there are no two persons who are alike here on earth, because they were created as individuals. They will be just as different in heaven and as different in their participation in heaven. This arises from the fact that sameness or identical repetition is a limitation. We know that if there existed such limitation or precondition of boundaries it would indicate that the power of the Creator, His variety of choices in the act of creation, is not infinite. And if the infinite is not infinite then it doesn't exist and we can forget about heaven — for without the infinite, according to the law of contradiction, there just isn't any heaven or hereafter. This lack of sameness is why we can say that a child, although it may have Aunt Susie's nose and "favor" its father, is not really identical to any other in the family — or to any other person anywhere. This is true not only naturally of the physical person but supernaturally of a person's perfection as a created human being.

Looking at all this from another aspect, we may protest that we really are not even our own original selves. For medical science tells us that every person's body is constantly being renewed, and that many of yesterday's cells have died and been replaced. This happens to every cell in the body, some say as often as every seven years. But we can reason that the Creator is directing the changeover, especially since we somehow *know* we are the same person we were ten or twenty or more years ago.

And in the Bible we read of the Creator's watch over us, sustaining us: "But you have mercy on all, because you can do all things; and you overlook the sins of men that they may repent. For you love all things that are and loathe nothing that you have made; for what you hated, you would not have fashioned. And how could a thing remain, unless you willed it; or be preserved, had it not been called forth by you? But you spare all things, because they are yours, O Lord and lover of souls" (Wis. 11:23-26).

We really can accept ideas that point to the unique individual's participation in heaven. These aspects will be taken up at greater length later. We may be accused of looking into a clouded crystal ball, but the reason for mentioning these aspects at this time is to emphasize the necessity to think in terms of the supernatural.

As remarked earlier, the one predominant drawback to getting a really clear idea of heaven is that we cannot completely disassociate our natural or human way of considering everything when we form our mental picture of heaven. We are further handicapped by having to use inadequate terms when speaking or writing about heaven. But isn't this true even of natural things about which we are really enthusiastic — when standing before a Grand Canyon view, a rainbowed sky, or a sunset — aren't we often "speechless" in awe? The publicity men who attempted to sound wildly enthusiastic about certain movies overworked their "super colossals" and "magnificents," thus making these superlative terms ineffectual.

We all have experienced the limitation of our language. Most often words fail us when we see an exceedingly beautiful sight or receive an unselfish act of genuine kindness or love. Our language just cannot keep pace with our perceptions or our emotions. But one thing is certain: don't for a moment think that because we must speak of heaven in imperfect human terms we are limiting it or cancelling any part of it. Heaven was never meant to square with our human ideas.

In our present state, the opposite is also true, that we make use of heaven as a measure for certain natural delights. We speak of a "heavenly kiss," the "blue heaven" of our dreams, and try in many ways to pull heaven down to our human level. This only tends to add confusion to confusion in all of the things we don't know about heaven. We should be cautious and realize that if we look into the mirror of nature we see darkly, if at all. But like corn which grows at night, we too can grow taller thinking our human thoughts of heaven, even in the darkness of our human nature.

On the other hand, from thinking humanly of heaven there arise many of our misconceptions of heaven as our final end and reward. Every human being is, by nature, possessed of desires which are infinite. They grow in a person like the delta of a great river — desire deposited upon desire until we can hardly envision the final growth. These infinite desires will be satisfied only in heaven in the realm of the supernatural — because this was the purpose in the will of the Creator — He created us to enjoy heaven. St. Augustine declares in his *Confessions*: "You have made us, O Lord, for Yourself, and our heart is restless until it rests in you."

What does this restless desire mean? It could be put this way: When someone makes an end-table or crochets a tablecloth, there is purpose in mind. With that purpose attained, we have created the object fully — we know what we made and for what purpose we made it. With man's destiny it is much the same: we have both purpose and end given to us by Him who made us. The entire multitude of natural things cannot satisfy our purpose, our desire. Only supernaturally can our purpose be attained, our desire be completely fulfilled. In desire, now we laugh at our yesterdays only in the brilliance of tomorrow. Aware of all our unrealized desires — we rejoice in our boundless hope.

The young boy who, walking along the midway of a state fair or the boardwalk of Atlantic City, exclaims with gastronomic exaggeration that he could "eat a million hot dogs," is attempting to express a huge appetite, an infinity of desire. Even knowing the vast, seemingly bottomless capacity of small boys, we still realize he is only expressing a wishful dream. It is the same with most of us when we think naturally of heaven. It is merely wishful thinking in which we apply our human imagination to our human desire and conjure up what we think would be the degree or amount of satisfaction. And it is in that "amount" that we make another mistake about heaven.

Heaven is not quantity. It is not the "mostest" of any one thing. This is merely a trick of our deluded, ever seeking but never satisfied mind. We can prove this wrong even on the natural level, for the man with the largest collection of phonograph records may not have the greatest appreciation and understanding of music. And it is quite evident that the man or woman with the most money is not the happiest individual, even if all that wealth is spent in satisfying his or her human desires. In heaven it is not at all a matter of having the most or taking the biggest portion. It is only the accepting of the happiness perfect for you and of your capacity to enjoy that perfectly because of your perfection.

We are most in error in thinking about heaven when we apply our human failings and faults to our wishful thinking about heaven. We kid ourselves into thinking that heaven will take revenge upon our enemies for us, that somehow the "score" will be evened out and in our favor. We wrongly think that heaven will take away something that someone else had and give it to us, thereby putting that someone at a disadvantage. In other words we are wrong in thinking that if all wars were refought in heaven everyone we chose, especially ourselves, would be victorious.

This comes from human-level thinking and the earthly, ambitious pastime of making every activity a form of contention. Our work, our games, and even our entertainment have this combative spirit. We are constantly struggling with others, trying to get ahead, be the first in line, acquire more "things" faster. But in heaven and for heaven, we are each contending with no one but ourselves. Heaven is, as St. Paul puts it, the prize that each one may gain in the race. Everyone comes in first in his own class and weight. And none of us would have it any other way, for we use our own energy — even while we may be helping others to use their energies better. We can share in the effort being made by those near us, and we can rejoice in receiving whatever aid they can direct toward our efforts.

Where do we stand now in our understanding of heaven? So far we have learned that we must look at heaven from a supernatural standpoint, free ourselves from thinking "naturally" about heaven, come to realize that we are capable of an infinite desire, that each one of us can and will enjoy heaven individually, uniquely. But most of all we have learned that heaven is not circumscribed or limited by our imagination or human limitations.

V

Eye hath not seen it, my gentle boy!
Ear hath not heard its deep songs of joy;
Dreams cannot picture a world so fair —
Sorrow and death may not enter there;
Time doth not breathe on its fadeless bloom,
For beyond the clouds, and beyond the tomb,
It is there, it is there, my child!
— Felicia D. Hemans, *The Better Land*

Aside from all we don't know about heaven because of our limited way of thinking, there are many things we do know — more than we even dreamed of previously in our cramped imagining. And, indirectly, scientific research is providing more and more knowledge to us, shedding further light on the ideas. That is one of the strange things about thinking about heaven — the bits that drop into place like jigsaw puzzle pieces, and we say to ourselves, surely I knew that, of course, it is all so reasonable.

The theologians, priests, and ministers, tell us all about heaven as the goal, the attainment of union with God through love. Often they are pulpit-pounding, table-thumping, speaking emphatically about how we may manage to get there. But they don't tell us too much about what heaven is like, nor do they tell us often enough to keep heaven ever before our minds and hearts. The Bible tells us we shall know God there because we shall see Him face to face. Death shall be cast down headlong forever says Isaiah (Is. 25:8), and he bids us all "awake and sing, you who lie in the dust" (Is. 26:19). And Thomas a Kempis, writing as the Lord would, declares: "Think, my son, on the fruits of your labors, of the end which will come soon, of the recompense and repose there in great joy. They cannot turn their heart to any other object, because, filled with eternal truth, they burn with charity which cannot be extinguished. They do not glory in their merits, because they do not attribute to themselves the good they have. They attribute it all to me, who has given them everything in infinite charity" (Bk. 11, ch. 49). And we can say simply, "Lord, when at last I see your face, I shall know the fullness of joy."

Science, which treats of the physical rather than the spiritual aspect, tells us about new facets of ourselves and gives us certain ideas about how we will enjoy heaven once we arrive there. So the sequence is: first the physical and then the spiritual, or first the natural and then the supernatural, just as we have reasoned all along.

Let us go back to the one essential condition we all know. Everyone must die to get to heaven. All during our lives we are deathly serious about heaven; after death, heaven is very serious about us. Now you may ask what science has to do with this essential. For one thing, science or scientists recognize that there is such a condition as death. The fact that science is seeking to prolong life does not indicate that it looks upon death as merely the accepted consequence of a bad illness. It may take a little time to determine just when the body is really dead — irreversible brain death, they call it now for want of a more confusing term. In fact, science, in its attempt to find ways and means of achieving longer life, is not trying to keep people in this world forever or make the insurance companies happier — perhaps it is really trying to give people more time to make up their minds to go to heaven.

In modern science, attempts have been made to deep-freeze a person until a cure is found for the cause of his or her death — the cryonics kick. This simply indicates that some scientists are fooling around with the impossible. They do not know the nature of death, the irrevocable finality of it, or they wouldn't be wasting their time.

One branch of science, a rather recent twig of the tree and surely one which has not fully grown, psychology and psychiatry, has been very little help in the quest for heaven. It fails because it argues for an identity of action in human behavior, attempts to pigeon-hole all individuals, and tries to disprove the before-mentioned idea that each one will enjoy heaven in a singular and individual manner. It is because of this like-behavior pattern that psychology and psychiatry claim to support, that they will never be exact sciences in the true sense of the word, for they can never arrive at a proven general law for every individual and for an indefinite number of different personalities. On the other hand, psychology and psychiatry have been helpful in determining certain reactions and in designating certain classifications of apparent identity that help us to know ourselves better. These classifications, such as the types of "-morphs," aid in understanding not *why* Johnny runs but *how* he runs; these give us insight into the progress we may make in understanding ourselves and, consequently, aid us in doing a better job of living in preparation for death.

Does it not seem strange that we all try to be quite exact and considerate about what we put into our wills, or "last testaments" as they are euphemistically called, but seldom do we assess what we might expect, deserve, or enjoy in heaven? We avoid making any attempt to know what might be awaiting us when we arrive there. Perhaps this is due to our lack of a developed faith. We depend on blind hope, not analysis. And while we hope "everything will turn out all right," we fumble along looking neither one way nor the other. Somehow we blunder through. Vague ideas suffice while we grimly admit for darn sure that we are going to die. A convicted killer declared, "All souls are headed for the same place, the land of no darkness. Some call it heaven." For someone to look no further than the "land of no darkness" seems an inadequate assessment. Being satisfied that anything more is beyond our thinking is taking entirely too dim a view.

The evangelist Billy Graham, in saying death "offers no fear at all, only anticipation.... I really believe I am going to a literal heaven," is expressing both faith and hope. He is able to understand that a vastly different life will be his and his alone.

A variety of other views on heaven are general in their appraisal, with few making any attempt at an analysis. Rev. Dr. G.L. Archer, professor of Old Testament at Trinity Evangelical Divinity School in Deerfield, Illinois, approves of an "absolutely literal" view like that given in the Book of Revelation in the Bible. This does not give much leeway for human reason nor for what we have learned of our own way of viewing enjoyment.

One Jesuit theologian speculated on the number of heavens we shall encounter, which he stated will be three: the heaven of today, existing without our present knowledge; the one which will exist after the parousia, or the second coming of the Lord Jesus; and the

"New Jerusalem" which is to be literally where the present city of Jerusalem stands and which will become the "religious center of the cosmos." These are not truly reasonable speculations as much as they are wild flings of fancy.

In all, there seems to be a reluctance to come to grips with what can be known reasonably about heaven. Even the poet's words, "heaven is the fitting room" where we try on various garments until we are arrayed in one of suitable "glory," seem only to recognize the diversity which is expressed by each person's having a unique heaven. This is much like the stone frieze in the medieval cathedral where small smiling figures rise from their tombs and draw on new hose and shoes to walk in the new land of the blessed.

These ideas are far from what modern man can learn even without fancy gadgets or computers. So departing for the present from the speculation of the worthy theologians, from science and the physical aspects, we may now consider more closely some of the spiritual or non-physical constituents that we know form heaven. This, I suppose, is where we really get confused with "the evidence of things not seen." If we consult the Bible, we find it quite a replete source of references about heaven. For instance, we learn that St. Paul had a pretty good idea of what heaven was to be like, not only for himself but for others also. Because of this he could quote Isaiah (Is. 64:3), with a kind of bland wonderment: "What eye has not seen, and ear has not heard, and what has not entered the human heart, what God has prepared for those who love him" (1 Cor. 2:9). Actually, St. Paul does not give us any details, but then he does not write as St. John did in the Book of Revelation. He does give emphasis to that very important prerequisite — love of God.

Two things we do learn from the Bible accounts: there will be *sound* and *light* in heaven. As the "angels sang," there must be music — and not just the "music of the spheres" the familiar phrase of poets. And there will be light — not just the "light of glory," but the light which does away with darkness because God created light. But this much we also know from reason, for God could not create the means of hearing music unless there was music to be heard. And the Creator could not create light and destroy it according to the law of contradictions as we understand it. We'll look at these later when we reason about our bodily senses.

We learn with some degree of assurance that heaven is going to be something sublime, because we realize that we have in our present form some limitations, some incapacities even in those capabilities we do enjoy. Paul does hint, however, that it is futile to a great extent even to speculate about the blessings of heaven because we can't come close to its reality. It will exceed even our wildest dreams and expectations.

While this is true, there is one point that we can deduce from St. Paul. It is: Heaven is one form of a "reward," something that is prepared or intended for all people. And the condition seems to be quite simple, at least at first glance, for the established condition is that we love God — which actually should be more easily done than said since He is lovable, He is love. It likewise should be clear to us that God is in heaven, it is there that He will be seen. Also, He has prepared heaven for someone — and it is only reasonable to assume that no one would get ready for company, for guests, by leaving home or by sweeping only an imaginary doorstep. Indeed, we *know* this, for we have long been praying "Our Father who art in heaven..." and everyone knows that this "Father" refers to God.

Looking deeper into the Bible, we get a still more definite idea of heaven. Christ referred to it in a variety of ways, in story, allegory, parable, assuring people again and again that there is a heaven and that it is to be enjoyed by them. There are biblical references concerning heaven as the "kingdom," as a "banquet," as the "new Jerusalem" — in fact, in just about every expression that would indicate what heaven is like, in terms easily understood.

But there is one reference, spoken of before, that substantiates, on interpretation, what we stated about each one of us enjoying heaven in our own particular, individual way. This we gather from the biblical description in which Christ, speaking obviously of heaven, said, "In my Father's house there are many dwelling places. If there were not, would I have told you that I am going to prepare a place for you? And if I go and prepare a place for you, I will come back again and take you to myself, so that where I am you also may be. Where [I] am going you know the way" (Jn. 14:2-4). This is, of course, figurative language, meant to make clear the loving intimacy His listeners might be able to comprehend. Christ almost drew them a picture — and some of them, like many of us, still did not understand what He was saying. We know He meant simply that there were "degrees" in heaven and that heaven would tolerate an infinite number of these according to the disposition of those who were to arrive. Heaven offers a diversity of place and depths of charity.

There are more facts about heaven we can learn from the Bible. For instance, that there are only a few who are present bodily in heaven. Primarily, one person is Jesus, whose body, say the theologians, has *locus*, or place, in heaven. This bit of heavenly information we get from the description of Christ's Ascension as recorded in the Bible. But even before this is the recounting of another event — the Transfiguration (Lk. 9:28-36) — which demonstrated a special epiphany, or manifestation to Peter, James and John of what heaven would be like, and it certainly gave them an inkling of how Christ was going to reign in glory. The three apostles were so impressed and mystified that they wanted to build structures or put up a marker to commemorate this event — a normal reaction for anyone experiencing the mystical and wonderful. It shows again the ongoing, forever and ever, liturgy which is ours. In other words, the apostles were overwhelmed, felt good and wanted to do something to express and hold this feeling. Instead, they were told not to speak for a time of what they had witnessed for they probably would not be believed, since they could not put into adequate words what they had actually seen.

Another person who many believe is bodily in heaven is the Virgin Mary, the Blessed Mother of God. Some question this, but their reasoning is difficult to understand. Certainly she lived and died and — had she not been taken to heaven — the apostles and many others who had great respect for her and were present at the time of her death would certainly have provided a well-marked tomb. But such has not been found by the most assiduous of archeological efforts, and we can safely say it is not likely to be found in the future. Aside from this, however, it is only reasonable to believe that she who by her purity and grace became the mother of the recorded God-man was specially deserving of heaven in body as well as soul.

The Bible grants us several other insights, glimpses, and previews of heaven. There is one given to Jacob in a dream wherein he sees a ladder or stairway with its top "reaching to the heavens" (meaning to a great height toward the sky) and angels were moving up and down on it (Gn. 28:12-13). Another is shown to Daniel where heaven is spoken of in terms of warfare and victory (Dn.7). And often the prophets, Isaiah, Jeremiah, David, Hosea, and others were told something of this wonderful place. Also, there is the lengthy, obscure view which St. John records in the Book of Revelation.

The one fact that becomes clear from all of these is that heaven has ever been presented in a "hidden" manner but in a way that the apostles and disciples could grasp, and we by our ability to interpret meanings, can also. The reason why we do not actually learn much about heaven from the accounts of the Bible is in our inability to perceive it fully. We are finite. We are limited. Nor is it possible to give each person a view of heaven just as he or she is going to enjoy it. Our knowledge will always be clouded in this our natural state, but our appetites can be whetted, so to speak.

Another generally held and fully believable piece of information about heaven is that it is the abode of great numbers of angels. They have been called the "messengers" of God, but their way of existing, their service, their abilities are not known. We have seen them pictured with wings, but it is most probably human fancy or man's limitations that add these props to beings that have by their nature no need for means of locomotion. Wings are as necessary to angels for "getting about" as walking sticks are to the wind. Angels, according to what the Bible and other reliable accounts tell us, are bodiless, pure spirits who have individual wills. How many are there? They are of a sufficient number and they are of an order of creation entirely different from that of mankind. Angels have specific functions they perform out of obedience, but this obedience is perfectly in accord with their own wills. In fact, we call them angels — which is a man-made tag describing their actions — because we know of them only in the role of messengers or as obedient beings. This in no way is to be confused with what a mother means when she says to Junior, "Oh, you are an angel for doing what I asked."

We have come to accept the statement that the place of human beings in heaven will be both greater than and distinct from that of angels. But this is reasonable because each person is, and will continue to be, an individual being of a different order of creation. Man will not be classified in a group or have a specific role as does each of the nine orders of angels. In addition humans will have a further distinction: the fullness, the wholeness of being present in heaven with both body and soul to experience the bliss. This does not detract from the greatness of all angels since they are distinct creations, different and separate in purpose and activity.

The angels in heaven have intuitive or immediate knowledge. They do not have to go the "reading, writing, arithmetic" way of us humans. While human beings have some intuition and possess certain psychological gifts, these are not the sources of our knowledge of heaven. We can only know what reason, based upon a wide experience and the recorded word which faith and tradition give us, permits us to adduce. To start a mere guessing game about heaven is not suitable or consoling for any of us.

Sometimes we read of pseudo-mystics who claim to have special information concerning life after death, but their statements have no religious authenticity or verifiable worldly knowledge. It is difficult to discern any truth in their imaginative accounts. Aware that today there seems to be a growing number of these pseudo-mystics about, and knowing that certain conditions must be fulfilled in both the spiritual and physical realms before credence can be placed in such "revelations," we can walk away from them — undisturbed emotionally or spiritually. The one who would truly prophesy about heaven must have followed a far different path than the publicity-seekers. Revelation is given to a person, God's "clay-sealed ark," only in the manner that God chooses.

At the same time, we do not wish to belittle or discard the accounts of genuine mystics who have been given special knowledge. Mystics, such as the prophets of the Bible, St. John of the Cross, St. Teresa, and others have been tested and accepted by the entire Christian community. Their revelation is part and parcel of the true revelation given to mankind, differing only in that it was intended for them especially, while what is revealed to us in the Bible is sufficient for anyone to embark on the pathway to heaven. The mysticism of these persons is on a high spiritual level, attested to by the degree of union with God which their prayer life and virtues attained. But their accounts are also highly personal. And here again these writings allow only a very limited and obscure insight into heaven as far as we are concerned, and they give us individually no more than the encouragement that heaven does await us. But this repeated assurance helps to bring our hope into full focus, and clears our vision for what we can see with our reason and accomplish with faith.

Among the things we know about heaven, two final points stand out. The first is the simple truth that one must die to go to heaven and that, in making the trip, no one will take anything with him. In Egyptian and Indian burials, it was the custom to inter with the body a goodly number of items which were thought to be useful to the departed. And these were unreasonable things, knowing heaven as we do — such trivia as extra thrones, gold ornaments, the tools of war, spears and arrows, flints, and all manner of choice personal items for the comfort of the deceased upon arrival at the "abode" or the "happy hunting grounds"! These never-to-be-needed and never-to-be-used things have served only as a rich supply of anthropological artifacts for our scholars to dig up and speculate about in their studies.

Also we must admit, there were gruesome aspects of ancient practices. According to their royal burial customs, the Egyptians sometimes supplied freshly killed slaves who were supposed to carry the load of things to be used by their deceased masters in the future life. This practice proved their ignorance of what heaven would be like — as did the custom of burying worthless tokens such as vials filled with tears shed at the bier on which the dead person was to look and be comforted.

Modern man has not gone to these extremes, being sentimentally content to make a gesture of dropping a choice ring or keepsake into the "last-journey" box. Such little goings-on, the flowers and wreaths, the make-up and piped-in music for the "resting place," are only symbolic. They have absolutely no bearing on one's entry into heaven. Fortunately, heaven will not be determined by what type of daisy blooms above a grave or what the remaining "friends" think of the departed. If a grand elegy were to be the password some would have to be rewritten — or as Shakespeare says, it is better to have a bad epitaph than an ill report given out while you live.

It is established and acknowledged that no one will carry worldly goods into heaven. It would not be possible to transport anything into the hereafter without first proving a lack of that something in heaven and thereby disproving heaven itself. Remember our law of contradictions — if heaven does not have everything or fulfill every desire it just simply will not be heaven.

All of this has a reasonableness beyond doubt. It is so because we come into this life with nothing, and what we are able to acquire by hard work is only a prop or adjunct to the human or "natural" in the equation "human Being." Thank heaven (to make a phrase the acknowledgement), there will be no need for "props" in the supernatural, and doubly thank heaven that we will not have to work and sweat as we have done here on earth to attain such things. Such encumbrances are not only unnecessary but they would be impediments — as they also frequently are while they are possessed on earth.

There is another reasonable aspect to this after-life empty-handedness. Who would want to take anything or even everything along — who would want to carry all his money if he had tons of it? If there were to be choices granted, say, of one or two items for each person to keep and carry, can you imagine what confusion would result? One would tug away at his television set, another would be pushing his Rolls-Royce, while a considerable number of the ladies would certainly opt for their mink coats. The fact that each one would have a particular preference is again confirmation that it does take a heaven to satisfy each. But no matter how attached one becomes, on the natural level, to natural things, the glue has not been invented that could make them stick together forever. It is all for the better that things which break and rust, are eaten by moths, recycled, or "reclaimed" by the finance company can be left behind with infinite satisfaction.

The second of these final known facts about heaven is that each person travels there alone. No matter how many are in the car at the frightful moment of impact, no matter how crowded the plane is when it plummets to earth, each one goes out strictly alone. There is no union or club to be joined, no travel agency that will guarantee companions, no insurance company to underwrite your accommodations, no lodge, association or social circle that will keep you from making the trip in any but a solitary manner. This too is reasonable. Anything that is shared, or jointly experienced, is diluted by the partition. And since each one will have a uniquely individual place in heaven, it would be impossible to condition that unique participation upon entry without limiting it and thereby destroying it entirely —

and destroying heaven. Besides, it is consoling to know that this aloneness is a condition of entering heaven. If, in being perfected, we have not each become self-sufficient in enjoyment to the infinite degree each one of us can sustain, then we have not been made as perfect as we can be.

Of all the aspects of human living in which humans are seen to be gregarious, not one will be manifest in dying. And in heaven there will be only uniquely different individuals sharing a special union with God in that state of being wherein perfect joy is experienced. Anything less would be a contradiction of perfectibility — and take away perfection and we're back to nothingness.

VI

Awake my soul! Stretch every nerve,
And press with vigour on;
A heavenly race demands thy zeal,
And an immortal crown.
— Philip Doddridge

Previously we remarked that even science has given us some insight into heaven. Science has not added to what we know of heaven by its usual direct method of exploration and examination, or its own empiricism. What science has added is a better knowledge of ourselves and, in doing so, it has opened up a wider field of speculation concerning heaven and our enjoyment there. Indeed, every new discovery concerning ourselves broadens the known possibilities of fulfillment which will be ours in heaven. Only in the broad sense that every science is directed more or less to a human being's greater understanding of himself can one say that all scientific study teaches us some aspect of truth as we will know and enjoy it in heaven. Perhaps this learning about ourselves is only discovery and definition, only clarification of what was always present in us; but even so, it makes for a rosier picture of anticipation when applied to speculation about heaven.

Today we explore the human psyche, the strange world of elements and particles, we increase our vision of the future. As we explore the macrocosm of outer space and the microcosm of the atomic universe, we may be able to get a better view of the infinite universe. It was not too long ago, as we record events, that the sun was considered the center of the firmament. We have advanced beyond our epicycled thinking to look at the atom, the meson, the baryons and the brief existence of the lawrencium. We have peered into the unseen darkness of outer space and the surfaces of planets. The laser is changing our world. All this has brought us to a new realization of the very womb of time, or made us at least reach the brink where "wonder is the basis of worship," as Carlyle said.

Before going into this phase of speculation, let us dispose of a few more suppositions and tag-ends of erroneous thought. Primarily we must energetically free ourselves from the assumption that there will be *time* in heaven. This is a most difficult but important exclusion. To grasp the idea that there will be no time in heaven demands a different process of reasoning — since it is almost impossible for humans not to think in terms of time. After all, it is one of our kinetic senses — the sense of time, the consciousness of yesterday, of today and tomorrow followed by yet another tomorrow. Franz Kafka wrote: "Only our concept of time makes it possible for us to speak of the Day of Judgement by that name; in reality it is a summary court in perpetual session" (*Letters*).

Someone once tried to demonstrate this absence of time in heaven by saying it is the "eternal now." The past has ceased to exist, the future will not begin to exist, and all that remains is the *now* forever. This mixes up our kinetic sense for we recognize that terms of before and after are themselves concepts of time.

"Time is a measurement of duration." We know this definition and accept it as fact. Also, time is a measurement of experience of delay, of intensity. This brings us to the crux of the relationship of God and time. Let us say at the outset: to wait for the future is impossible for God because this is an imperfection of degree. From this we say we will not await a future once we are in heaven. Yet a certain degree of the human element in heaven *must* include a kind of progressing growth in the contemplation of God, for if we were not to have our changing human personality in heaven we would become static, frozen in our state of bliss. Thus we can reason that being timeless and/or having absolute simultaneity could only result in immutability and not having a change for the better from the human to the super-human.

We try to simplify the picture by thinking of time as measurement, which it truly is — the interval between a beginning and an ending, between one heart beat and the next, any series of changes marked by degrees of duration. Roughly, we can deduce that since the condition of heaven is eternal, therefore without beginning or end, it cannot be thought of as an interval at all because the two poles of measurement do not exist. Besides, measurement brings into our thinking the ideas of intensity, duration, value, or comparison — the brighter, longer, better, or bigger idea of something. And a perfect good cannot be subject to measurement. Moreover, the perfect heaven itself will not be measurable, as there will be no degrees or convenient markers by which we could attempt a measurement. In other words, there will be no sunrise, sunset, solstices, lunar periods, light years or the like by which we could gauge a portion of being in perfection. That's it — we'll be there, but time won't be. There is no such thing as a little bit dead. Even now we are relating to heaven, for earthly life begins immortal life and we are on our way, proceeding toward perfectibility.

Then, too, there will be no qualification in heaven, qualification being a concept of measuring. We often say, for instance, when we've had an especially good experience, "That's the best time I've had in all my life!" which is measuring by comparison one period or experience against our memory of other experiences. We are continually doing this, weighing our sensory impressions or sensations against a standard which looms up in time; everyone has his or her own Greenwich time in memory. But, remember, in heaven you won't have to bother with similarities or dissimilarities, U.S. standards or metrics — the one perfect degree is exclusive of all comparisons.

With all methods of measurement, science can give us an approximation of time's duration, and knowledge of suspended laws of gravity in space — but science is not able to give us a *perfect* zero, or infinity.

All this may sound like vague rationalizing, like trying to perceive a scent in a vacuum. But there is an eminent hint of truth in this mood of wonder, since we wish to take a look at what the sensory pleasure or delight or enjoyment of heaven will be, since we now understand and enjoy the sensual pleasures of being human. Without time, the function of our senses takes on a different aspect. As things are here and now, time is a notable contributory condition to our sensory pleasure. It takes the eye about one tenth of a second to see. Between the touch of lips on lips and the soaring of emotion or passion there is a small lapse of time. Even our ears are not immediately beguiled by dulcet tones of music — or as anyone knows, a small boy's response to his mother's call may take ages. We hear a dull preacher and think he drones on forever. Also remember, time introduces an element of fatigue in our human acts — the longer one does something, even holding hands, the more wearisome it becomes, instead of more enjoyable. Time can limit, flatten, or intensify, but primarily it joins with judgment to bring comparisons into our sensory perceptions. "It looked so good yesterday, why does it seem so banal and trivial today," says the dilettante.

Taking things in their proper order, we cannot immediately start with an examination of our bodily senses in the effort to understand heaven. Everyone (we use this term inclusively) agrees that after the cessation of time — that is death, the body is put away; and let's assume everyone agrees that the soul proceeds into immortality. For, were it not immortal, the soul at death would be like a last breath of air because it is entirely spiritual and needs the bodily confines to give it an understandable reality. The soul has not been seen, nor felt, nor examined under the most powerful microscope. Yet the soul has certain faculties that distinguish it from other spiritual substances or properties. It is not simply like the fragrance of the rose.

Primarily, the soul has the triune faculties of *understanding, will,* and *memory* which all might be called intellectual faculties, and these unique powers will gain us heaven's most glorious delights. The ability to think proves a soul more than other reasonings. Once a very learned and elderly historian, after discoursing on notable men and women of the past, was addressed by one of his listeners who said, "Your knowing so much of these great people will surely make your heaven a glorious place for renewing acquaintance with them." To which the historian replied, "No — I'll be much too occupied learning the infinite truths of their Creator."

We may find obscurity when we try to place a yardstick beside such intangibles; but faint heart never won heaven. It is no place for the unheroic, and missing by a million miles in our speculation is still close enough when we're dealing with infinity. For certain, heaven is not going to be just a fleeting glimpse of glory. It is going to be a real participation, a "partaking" in glory itself. Those who falsely claim that they will return to earth and will be some animal or thing or someone else, realize little about the nature of the soul or the glorious participation that each is destined to enjoy in heaven.

For a moment we will have to look a little more deeply into heaven. Thus far we have arrived at the point where the soul is in heaven. We know that the soul is a spiritual being with faculties of memory, understanding, and will that enable it to delight in heaven to the fullest. God is the center, the essential of heaven. There's no getting around that in our thinking. It's the truth and that's all there is to it. As the Psalmist says so eloquently:

"Whom else have I in heaven?

"And when I am with You, the earth delights me not.

"Though my flesh and my heart waste away,

"God is the rock of my heart and my portion forever" (Ps. 73:25-26).

And St. Augustine spoke of that fire of desire, proclaiming: "Late have I loved You, O beauty so ancient and so new, late have I loved You ... You breathed fragrance upon me, and I drew in my breath and do now pant for You; I have tasted You and do now hunger and thirst for You. You did touch me and I burned for Your peace. When once I shall be united with You with all my being, there shall be no more grief and toil, and my life shall be alive, filled wholly with You."

Heaven is God's home. It is our home. We know the Father, God. We pray to Him. Home is where the family is; if the persons who make up the family are not there, there is no heaven — but it cannot be and not be, as we know. Further, God is spirit, and the soul being spirit also will be united with God in a union, a bond, which is much closer than that between two relatives, friends, or lovers, and exceedingly closer than the "brotherhood" between the members of an organization.

It is especially through the triune faculties of the soul, intellect, will, and memory, that this close union with God will be brought about. We wouldn't want it any other way, even though it is difficult to grasp because even in life it is by means of these faculties that humans achieve their greatest degree of earthly perfection. Now how does this union happen in heaven? Quite simply, for through these faculties we will know God as He is, and knowing Him fully at last will be such great joy, such infinite delight, that it will be heaven itself. As St. John says, "...we are God's children now; what we shall be has not yet been revealed. We do know that when it is revealed, we shall be like him for we shall see him as he is" (1 Jn. 3:2). And St. Paul declares: "...but we will all be changed, in an instant, in the blink of an eye, at the last trumpet. For the trumpet will sound, the dead will be raised incorruptible, and we shall be changed. For that which is corruptible must clothe itself with incorruptibility, and that which is mortal must clothe itself with immortality" (1 Cor. 15:51-53).

First, through the faculty of *understanding*, by which our soul will have an immediate knowledge of God, we will experience joy. This is not ordinary joy, the pleasure of having things or desires satisfied, but the joy which Yeats calls the "joy of wisdom." There will never be a failure that will diminish it, like the light from a guttering candle, nor will there be a need to study this joy in order to expand it. Instead this knowledge will be complete and perfect for each of us. Some might think this small recompense for giving up some of the good things of earth. We can only say that this knowledge of God, this experience of true completeness, the fullness of joy will be ineffable reward and total heaven. Why? Well, because it is, humanly speaking, gratifying to know a thing; and there is great satisfaction in knowing anything completely. But to have a grasp of all knowledge at its source is such a tremendous good that we cannot even imagine its extent, its constant intensity. To find a nugget of gold is good; to find the "mother lode" is better; to find the very source of all gold is certainly best. The poet Phoebe Cary says: "And every dream we thought was lost / In heaven shall be fulfilled."

This knowledge or understanding of God is the primary good to be sought. It is where men have failed often in this life. As we read in the Book of Wisdom: "For all men were by nature foolish who were in ignorance of God, and who from the good things seen did not succeed in knowing Him who is, and from studying the works did not discern the artisan; but either fire, or wind, or the swift air, or the circuit of the stars, or the mighty water, or the luminaries of heaven, the governors of the world, they considered gods. Now if out of joy in their beauty they thought them gods, let them know how far more excellent is the Lord than these, for the original source of beauty fashioned them" (Wis. 13:1-3).

The second faculty of the soul for experiencing God is *will*. It is through *will* that love is expressed — a "going toward." It is through *will* that God as *Love Itself* will be experienced. It is through our will that we have the ability to express love, true charity, the greatest of the three virtues of faith, hope, and love. However, in heaven, coming to know God is the reason for the soul's will to express love; and, since the object of love is the good, and since God is all goodness, He is supremely loved immediately upon being seen and known. If there is joy in loving on earth, there is infinite joy in loving Love Itself in heaven. Someone may say, "This will be like having the miracle of love happening every day!" True. But as the humorist Mr. Dooley ruefully remarked, "Miracles are laughed at by a nation that reads thirty million newspapers a day and supports Wall Street!" But there are people among us who do find time to think of God and love Him. For these the first of God's commandments is a serious matter, for God has commanded us to love Him with our whole heart and soul, mind, and strength.

Through its third faculty, *memory*, the soul is going to delight in heaven. This is not memory in the sense that we recall pleasant things or events of the past. (And isn't it strange that you find it easier to remember nice things that have happened to you than to recall painful experiences?) Actually, in heaven, the spiritual memory flows out of the knowledge of God, and the will to Love itself. It is the link between understanding or knowledge and will. It gives so to speak, an extra power or voltage to the other two faculties. For example, have you ever put before you a perfectly ripened fruit, one without flaw or blemish or dryness? If so, you will know that you can taste it even before you bite into it, the anticipation is that of goodness. And when you are eating it you are filled with delight — you literally love it. Now, after the fruit has been consumed, you can still, if you want to, think of and love that fruit, and enjoy its goodness again and again. Even if immediately after eating you were made hungry again, you would be able to experience the joy again most intensely. That's somehow the way your faculty of memory is going to work in heaven. It will be like being drained and immediately refilled again without becoming aware of the draining and filling, for there will be no lapse of time in between, and so the joy of infinite knowledge and love of God will be made additionally gratifying in an unending sequence of immediate and continuous joy.

This singular enjoyment of the spiritual is, of course, never experienced on a natural plane. Even if we repeat a pleasure, it never seems quite the same the second or third time around. Thus we have no means of comparison between the font of goodness and the goodness itself. Some mystical writers and others call this ultimate union with God, the seeing of God in the fullness of His eternal glory, the *Beatific Vision*. St. Augustine expressed it best when he said of God's simplicity and infinite goodness in being pure spirit: "What He has, that He is. He is outside of time, so that all time lies before Him in an eternal present, a *Now* that is in itself the 'beginning and the end,' the Alpha and the Omega. (Rev. 1:8) Every act of God speaks of His attributes, His every perfection." In heaven you will have knowledge and understanding without study or reasoning — total recognition of God. In heaven you will know *love* in the will without direction or planning; being led without adverting to obedience or law — you will totally love God Who is Love.

St. Peter tells us of the summation of these three faculties of the soul and how we will be transformed by their exercise in heaven. He says we "come to an inheritance that is imperishable, undefiled, and unfading, kept in heaven for you" (1 Pt. 1:4). A truly frightening but infinitely wonderful fulfillment which we poor mortals cannot, sad to say, fully appreciate now.

Others writing of the sight of God, the Beatific Vision, simply describe it as heaven — the end all and be all of living, the joy to be experienced by the immortal soul forever. To try to represent this spiritual grasp of heaven graphically and put it into human terms is just not possible. The best we can say is that the faculties of the soul, the intellect and its powers of will and memory, are the greatest things that we can boast about, and when these become perfected it will be almost beyond any belief what a tremendous, unutterably wonderful joy it will be.

In this life, the soul is commonly belittled. Any stroll down one of our streets will show you the importance showered upon the puny "creations" of man, the "glories" that man erects for the comfort of the body and in praise of the body, to the confusion of the soul through pride. Whoever bows down before the world is deceived time and time again. As the poet Richard Wilbur wrote, "We milk the cow of the world, and as we do/ We whisper in her ear 'You are not true.' " But in heaven the order is reversed. There the soul comes into its rightful place as the great "in-His-likeness" creation of God. And the soul's God-like greatness will be seen with wonder because of this likeness.

When eventually united with the body, the soul will be able to receive new pleasure because of this union with the glorified body. The soul will then grow to the fullness of its use of faculties and its emotional and sensitive nature. For the soul's delight, the glorified senses will empower it to receive the joys which come through all of the bodily senses. Further, the soul will be made more perfect because of the union with the body, for the glorified body will be subject to the soul and will perfect all its intellectual operations. This will be vastly different from earthly existence where "the corruptible body burdens the soul and the earthen shelter weighs down the mind that has many concerns" (Wis. 9:15).

Next, we come to the participation of the body in heaven. How about the body rising and being incorruptible? What will it be like? Truly our bodies will be transformed, immortal, spiritualized, incorruptible, no longer subject to suffering. It is amazing how many times we read in the Bible that the body will be glorified, so many that we may be reasonably assured the "glory" will be indeed the new condition of the body in heaven. This is not to say that the body we will have in heaven will be exactly the same one we had on earth. We know that our body, made of moisture, chemicals, and transitory elements, changes even during our lifetime. That is, its cellular existence is modified and replenished often throughout our natural lives so that the physical substance varies.

It would seem that the souls of those who have died in past centuries, as well as those of the recent dead, are all awaiting this event, the resurrection, and that there is an interval of time between the arrival of the soul in heaven and of the body's coming to join it there. But the soul in heaven does not have to deal with time, and whatever the interval may be before the soul and the body are reunited, it will certainly seem like no time at all.

While we cannot boast of too much knowledge about the soul, we do know a considerable amount about the body. We know how to use it and abuse it. We know it is a well designed machine that functions under the most adverse conditions, that it is a chemical factory, self healing, a conglomerate, that it can give us a good deal of pleasure and quite a few twists of pain. We have learned that the body is made up of thirty of the one hundred plus fundamental elements we have identified as of today, and the most basic of these is carbon. (There will be other elements, fractions thereof, or particles discovered as science continues to progress.) We discover new facts about the body almost every day. But at the same time we know that, for the body, heaven is not just a matter of a plunging skyline. It is the body which dies but, eventually, since it shares in the "person" of this creature called a human being, it too will enter, though changed, into heaven. In other words each person will be body and soul in heaven.

This concept of the body being in heaven is difficult to grasp — but we must free ourselves from thinking of our body as it was or is at only one particular time. To stand still is physically impossible, for medical science has demonstrated the constant cellular changes that take place as the body of an individual grows and ages. Likewise we know of transplanted organs, tissues from our body living in that of another person. The way to consider this in all reasonableness is for us to look upon the body from the Creator's view — God does not bestow to only one body a measured material, a certain quantum, per person, since this would be a limitation of His power as Creator. Nor does He allow only one season's foliage to a tree in the lifetime of the tree. We do learn from St. Paul that the body will be changed — glorified, but what that glorification of the body will be is not known to man.

Many years ago, Aristotle, who was both a thinker and an observer, wrote that man has five senses: taste, touch, sight, smell, and hearing. These we recognize by their use. If one or other is flawed we consider it a handicap. We discover these to be our basic tools whose operation depends upon physical organs that respond to stimuli to which they are naturally receptive. Modern scientists go a step further. They name these five the basic external senses, then go on to list an array of internal senses which they call kinesthetic. These senses are more related to nerve-endings and the sensation we experience in bodily motion or positioning, thus responding to movements of the body through its muscles, tendons, and joints. There is now a science of kinetics.

Over and above the external and internal senses, modern science also refers to a wide range of emotional senses, such as "sense of fear," "sense of well-being," and the like. To these we have corresponding senses that are more related to the intellectual life and are referred to as senses of the mind, such as "sense of humor," "sense of estimation," "sense of time." These latter are the inorganic means by which we "sense" where we are or how we are oriented in relation to other realities. All of these senses form the sentient human being. They do not all fit the same definition of course, but they do make up the totality of function which belongs to the oneness of an individual, and they make up the totality of function which belongs to the body united with the soul as well.

When the resurrected body arrives in heaven it will bring its tools with it. Otherwise the principal would have been annihilated along with the parts and this would be a contradiction of the creative powers of the Creator. Thus we may ask, what happens to the body, to our senses? Well, we know the body will be changed, that it will be "glorified." The word means little to us as a description of a condition. But examined more closely it comes out like this: "filled with glory." Going a step further, maybe we can find a clue to how the "glory," the supernaturalization happens.

To exemplify this in a limping manner, we have said that a body is matter, a combination of substances. To simplify this further, we can consider one element of matter as found in nature ... let's take carbon. When it is chemically changed, crystallized, carbon becomes a diamond and is exceedingly more beautiful and valuable than coal, for instance, which also is carbon. You might say the carbon was filled with glory in becoming a diamond. Something like that is the change which takes place in the body on its entering heaven. At any rate, it is certain that a glorified body will be a perfected body, a body radiant, purified, a body whose functions will be expanded to a perfect degree of operation.

The Bible doesn't help us here a great deal, but St. Paul, writing to the early Christians of Colossae, told of the change from the natural state of things: "These are only a shadow of what is to come; but the substance belongs to Christ. Let no one disqualify you, insisting on self-abasement and worship of angels, taking his stand on visions, puffed up without reason by his sensuous mind, and not holding fast to the Head, from whom the whole body, nourished and knit together through its joints and ligaments, grows with a growth that is from God.

"If with Christ you died to the elemental spirits of the universe, why do you live as if you still belonged to the world? Why do you submit to regulations, 'Do not handle, Do not taste, Do not touch' (referring to things which all perish as they are used), according to human precepts and doctrines?" (Col. 2:20-22 — Revised Standard Version, Thomas Nelson & Sons, Ltd.).

The body in heaven will indeed be something special. From being a creation in nature, it will be "supernaturalized," brought to that perfection which is the purpose for which it was created. Now, this is not just "a word from our sponsor." It means that all properties, functions, and natural endowments will be perfected. It means that the resurrected body, united again with the soul in heaven, will make up the whole person, the entire being, and that soul and body together will enjoy in perfection and to perfection the indescribable delights of heaven. And the body will be united to the soul, we know, because they are two creations joined to form one complete person, the material, physical body and the spiritual soul. To separate these in a teleological sense would be to destroy what the Creator has made as an inseparable entity — to annihilate either one would be a contradiction of the creative power and hence would deny that power itself.

Throwing the beam of reason's light more sharply on this, we find a few questions which arise immediately out of our simplicity. What will the age of the body be in heaven? (And here again we speak in human terms of development in time.) Will it be youthful, coltish, teenaged, mature like a "man of distinction," or old and sagacious as a senior citizen? Rest assured! The body will neither creep nor dodder into heaven. Everyone there will be at the perfect age which might be arrived at by human calculation. It will be that age when all growth, all maturing, has arrived at its proper and highest peak and just before the decline sets in. Some place this age at twenty-eight years; some say it is just a shade one side or another of thirty; and others, using the biblical age of Christ at the time of His death, place this closer to thirty-three. Here admittedly we are in an area of pure speculation, but we reasonably can agree that this age is definitely not forty, the so-called life-beginning age. Again, humanly speaking, we know the body enjoys a time when it seems to be well-attuned, when each movement and act of the mind seems to be at its best and we can project that this will be the acme of heavenly existence as well, but never-ending. This is the age which will be the norm of the body in heaven, the constant age of the body's perfection.

It must also be supposed that when the body is in heaven it will require its ordinary property of movement. However, movement will be accomplished without the drawback of earthly life, namely, the effort to move about that walking or running demand. Rather, movement will be immediate — the supernatural body will be of an order which is unrelated to space, hence it will not be controlled or limited by spatial considerations.

Another question arises from just plain human curiosity: will there be bow-legs, cross-eyes, etc. in heaven? At ease, all of you who suffer the slip-ups of nature. If there were such conditions in heaven, any blemish, mark, or crippling, they would be like penalties — in themselves a contradiction of the idea of perfection. Nor would any impairments be considered "marks" of distinction as they can be in our human thinking. Also, the condition of the body will not be according to anyone's passing preference no matter how many times your hair was dyed while on earth. Instead the body will be in that state of perfection which means every faculty, every natural possession will be perfected in the most marvelous realization of the unique qualities of each one's creation.

No, there will be no flaws, afflictions, or bad effects from having abused nature by wearing size fives on nature's eights. In fact, even those with an excised appendix, or with an amputated digit will be back to normal with the perfect wholeness of the natural body. The conditions the body suffers in this earthly state of imperfection, which conditions are manifestations of imperfection, will not continue into the life hereafter.

An objection might arise. With everyone being of a like age, whole and sound, might there be a monotony of sameness? Remember what was said earlier, that each person is a singular creation and will be perfected as an individual. It might be likened to a maple tree in autumn. We don't say each leaf is beautiful but that the tree is beautiful — yet each leaf taken by itself is a thing of beauty whose individual glory is given over to the beauty of the entire tree. All persons in heaven will be beautiful in themselves and together they will form the beauty of heaven's harmony of grandeur. There can be no lack of grandeur or it would not be heaven.

This individuality of perfection will be even more pronounced in the degrees of glory that will further distinguish each person in heaven due to the merit achieved on earth. There will be no monotony possible, since monotony is a limitation which is impossible in heaven. Instead there will be an infinitude of characteristic demarkations, an endless variety.

As an interlude of caution we must say that not every person will enjoy heaven in the same way as every other person. No, there will be a differentiation between persons because of their merit. This means that there is as much difference between the splendor of the sun as reflected in an emerald and as sparkling in a diamond. This is not an essential difference but one of degree. St. Augustine compares it to a man and a boy, each having a new suit of clothes: the boy is not less happy because he has less cloth in his suit than the man, but he is happy to be clothed and have his own suit. The Bible says "star differs from star in glory."

The distinction arises partly from the talents and gifts a person has, but chiefly from how these are used in the service of God. It is the consoling reward of virtue — and this is the only way we would have it. For, while everyone may hear the music at a concert, those who have studied music can appreciate it fully, while those who have shied away from the effort of study can enjoy it only to a lesser degree.

To be considered now are two special features of the glorified body — the real topping-off of your crowning glory. They concern the presence of the body in heaven. These are the facts: that the body in heaven will never suffer and that it will be incorruptible, and will never lose its glory nor even have it diminished. The reasons for these conditions are almost obvious. The first, the body's non-suffering in heaven, is called impassibility. It means freedom from pain, from suffering, freedom from one's own ability to cause oneself to suffer. But it does not mean that one loses the capability of having or enjoying pleasure. The glorified body is not such that nature is destroyed but that it is perfected. The human body was not created to suffer but to experience the good that God intended to give each person as a created right, a right following upon creation.

On earth, we suffer under the events of life and by our own folly. We become, willingly at times, our own enemies, making our bodies pay dearly for overindulgence and lack of self-control, for obstinate resistance to the good. In heaven our senses will be perfected and we will not suffer through them because the law of life will be changed to heaven's law of the supernatural where all is in perfect harmony with the will of the Creator. It would be unthinkable that any degree of suffering could be present in this bliss because, if any were imposed or could be induced, the suffering would have to be perfect and that would mean a serious contradiction, for having perfect pain and perfect happiness at the same time is not possible, as we have learned.

Nor will we suffer because of our own stupid actions which in life seem to have both immediate and delayed consequences. The human body on earth is subject to the laws that govern matter, the substance of bodily life. Deterioration, disease, aging — all bring on illness and pains. The perfected body, however, will no longer be conditioned or limited. The very idea of heaven's reward alone could not be sustained under a law which would permit even the most gradual withholding or diminution of any good or any capability. If this were so, it would mean a further penalty for man and this is intolerable to imagine in a perfected state of being, which moreover, will last forever.

That the body is incorruptible follows from much the same reasoning. Only in nature's law are things of matter corruptible, subject to change, decay, rust, and death. In the supernatural, the body is incorrupt as St. Paul states, and in the presence of Love itself as found in the Creator, we will be able to say with St. Augustine: "All within us cries out: 'we made not ourselves, but the Eternal One made us.' If, after this word, all things were silent, and He Himself alone would speak to us, no longer through them, but by Himself: if then our soul, lifting itself on the wings of thought up to eternal wisdom, could retain unbroken this sublime contemplation: if all other thoughts of the spirit had ceased and this alone had absorbed the soul, and filled it with joy, the most intimate and most divine: if eternal life resembled this ravishment in God which we experience for a moment: would this not be the consummation of that word: 'Enter you into the joy of your Lord?' "

It is strange, but there are many who would like to set a gauge of their own for heaven. And if it fails to come up to their preconceived idea, they don't want any part of it. They would limit it to what they like now, and whatever they frown on they would eliminate from heaven. They think of humans and their senses in the restrictive understanding of their own limitations, squint at abuses and cry, "Naughty, naughty," and say there must be some curtailment of the enjoyment of heaven for others. These are the "treacle tricklers," the sweetness-and-light crowd, who point to the "primrose path" and want others to end up with only a single flower if any at all. They are as bad in their lack of compassion, putting restrictions on heaven as the "bluedomers" who claim the sky is the limit, that anything goes. Once and for all it can be flatly stated: joy will be unconfined! Each one of the senses of every person, all essentially a part of human nature, each will be perfected and fulfilled.

In human life the reception of stimuli — sounds, colors, tastes, odors, caresses — are dependent upon the external organs. If these organs are defective or absent we do not enjoy the sensations they are designed to convey. In heaven, enjoyment of the senses will not be dependent upon these external organs. This would be too limiting, because our organs are imperfect in many instances. Sense perception in the human person will be glorified, that is, it will not function as we experience it now. In the resurrected body we will receive sensory joy — but not according to the limits of the sense organs. The transmission of sight, sound, taste, smell, and touch will be made through the soul and faculties of the mind immediately. Were these to be transmitted in heaven as they are under nature's law, through wave-lengths, contacts, or material substances or gases, it would introduce measurement or limitation into heaven and this is impossible.

The senses of the human body are not just superfluous appendages which are possessed in life to serve a "living" purpose. They are not mere accidents but are essential to human nature. Thus we can say, humanly speaking, that a blind or deaf person is not a perfect human receptive unit because something which is essential to the integrity of the human body is lacking to him. Glory destroys nothing that is natural to the body, but perfects it. Consequently all senses will be raised to their full perfection, and the blind will see, the deaf will hear. Their activity and power of perception of the senses will be extended to the full purpose of their nature and they will convey to the soul all the forms of delight and pleasure which they are capable of in their perfection.

As in nature, the recognition and enjoyment of sensory impressions are not in the organ itself, so in heaven the pleasure will be immediate and experienced in the mind and soul. Also, there will be no instinctual acts necessary in heaven, life will not have to be nourished, preserved, or propagated, since these are associated with the animal nature shared by man. Nor will one's life in heaven ever be in jeopardy, so the instinctual and reflexive actions of self-preservation will be unnecessary. Here we speak of these organs of sense as they are known in our human experience, but in heaven we will be concerned only with the result of sense perception — immediate joy.

Science has told us much about our senses and has demonstrated that the external senses of the human being on earth have limitations. For example, in the diffraction of light the spectrum shows a range of colors from deep purple to intense red. This is similar to the range of colors the eye sees in the sky opposite the sun in the refractive dispersion of sunlight which we call a rainbow. The spectrum of colors can be seen by the naked eye and often many degrees of intensity are distinguishable. Yet it has been shown in the laboratory, in observing the spectra of light and energy, that the eye does not record and transmit to the brain for recognition all of the colors in light. For example in photographing the diffraction of light on film, there is an extended banding in shades of grey which indicates that many colors are present that the eye does not recognize.

This definite limit in the range, the receptivity of the human eye, is also found in the other organs of hearing and taste. However, in heaven there will be no limit to the perfected sense of vision. Eyes will register all possible colors in light, for one of the known essential features of heaven is the quality of light — "a man clothed in light," for example. Light free of any accidental cause, light that needs neither sun, candles, nor the energy of electricity — simply light created as a condition without the necessity of material means of transmission. This will be light without the glare of brightness that blinds. There will be no neon jungles, no glitter nor reflections, no turning on and off of lights.

The result of this is natural — there will be no shadow, no darkness. For, where light is at its very source, perfect, surrounding and compenetrating all, there can be no absence of light (darkness), and no interference with light (shadow), else there would be limitation and such limitation would mean measurement and degrees and would thus destroy perfection. One cannot have light and no light at one and the same instance — no light (or darkness) would be the same contradiction of perfection. It follows, then, that heaven will be a very colorful place, free of any of the drab or tell-tale greys that limit our present pleasure in the use of our sense of sight. The expanded perception of the possible colors seen in the diffraction of light will make heaven a beautifully colorful place indeed.

From very early times the Irish have had a blessing that recognizes the quality of light: "May the blessing of light be on you, light without and light within." It is this fullness of light of which we think when we approach the truth of the presence of light in heaven.

It has also been demonstrated by science that colors have psychological effects, or that a color inspires a distinct sensation in response to its intensity. There are colors which please and those which excite while others have a soothing effect. This is a communication between the external and internal senses. The color coordinator is aware of the effects of color, the harmony of a blend of colors. Something like a shudder of horror goes through one with the resultant "clash" when a person sees cousin Mabel arrayed in orange and purple, or Johnny in the "hot pink" tie that Auntie Mame gave him. But tasteful color combinations cause a pleasurable reaction. In being given the capability to perceive the perfection and infinite variety of all the colors of heaven, the mind will experience infinite delight over and above the joy of seeing the colors. This will result in the added sensation of euphoria that harmonious colors give to a person.

With the sense of hearing there is a similar expansion of joy that we may look forward to in heaven. We know that the human ear is capable of catching only certain wave lengths, that beyond the range of our sound reception there is an infinitude of other sounds and harmonies. We have also experienced that in our present state, sonics can be productive of pain and disorientation of all our senses. One instance of the broader range of sound has been observed to a limited degree with the dog-whistle as it emits a sound which Fido hears, but which is pitched too high for the human ear to receive. In heaven, where we know there is sound, the perfected sense of hearing will be able to receive infinite acoustical ranges in perfect harmony and without deleterious effects. There will, of course be no strident sounds, no caterwauling, no noise — since noise, disharmony, is an imperfection or misuse of sound. The music of heaven, which some call the "music of the spheres" and others picture naively as angels with harps a-twang, will be the ultimate in pleasurable appeal to the sense of hearing.

There is surely the sound of happy music in heaven — happier than any madrigal. We read of it in the Bible in the last Psalm: "Praise him with the blast of the trumpet, praise him with lyre and harp, praise him with timbrel and dance, praise him with strings and pipe. Praise him with sounding cymbals, praise him with clanging cymbals." And for those who are not attuned to instrumentals, it is reassuring to read that "the angels sang," on the night we annually celebrate as the Lord's birthday.

Expansion of the senses of seeing and hearing will be infinite in heaven. The same is true of the other senses. Every sense will act according to its nature — that is, according to the object for which it was intended to act. This, however, does not mean that there will be food in heaven, yet there will be the ancillary sense of the smell of food. While there will be the sensation of caresses of a physical nature or the pleasure of sex, there will not be indulgence in sex per se. Now some will raise an eyebrow at these declarations, and those with the *Playboy* attitude will shrug and choose to go elsewhere. That is their privilege. But the simple truth of logic is that no single sense of the human body will be without function, and all the senses will be rewarding — since to deny them would be punishment. However, there is the danger that we may regard eating, or drinking, or sleep, or sex as necessary when we know that by their very nature these belong only to the animal life of human persons. Food is necessary to sustain human life, not supernatural life. Yet the pleasure of food, the taste, fragrance, and variety of such sense delights will be apprehended as a present and everlasting good in heaven.

The same facts are true of the senses of touch and scent and the pleasures of bodily responses. It must be evident that these functions in our human nature have a purpose which is no longer necessary for sustaining or maintaining our supernatural lives. Food will not be necessary because there can be no hunger or need for growth. The sense of smell in our basic natural life is primarily for protection from offensive or harmful things, as well as being for pleasure. Touch is also for protection, as when touching a hot stove or sensing frostbite, but such protective measures are not necessary in heaven. Sex and its syndrome of carnal pleasures is, humanly speaking, purposeful for the desire to reproduce life and the continuation of the species. Such a continuation will no longer be necessary. But, and this is the true purposeful activity of the presence of senses in heaven, there will be the attendant pleasure or pleasurable sensations that come to us through these senses. Too often in life we confuse the pleasure with the need; we overindulge in eating not because we are hungry but because we salivate at just seeing an advertisement for food. It is easy to abuse appetite.

When we turn to the Bible we hear Christ declare: "You are misled because you do not know the scriptures or the power of God. At the resurrection they neither marry nor are given in marriage but are like angels in heaven. And concerning the resurrection of the dead, have you not read what was said to you by God, 'I am the God of Abraham, the God of Isaac, and the God of Jacob'? He is not the God of the dead but of the living" (Mt. 22:29-32). And as His listeners were dumbfounded, we too are filled with wonder. We do not know how, but we know that the reasonable truth is that the senses are perfected there according to the true purpose for which they were created.

We know that it is in the mind, not in the sense organ itself that we recognize and interpret the stimuli given to us. Some senses are even interdependent to a degree, as is true in the close association of smell and taste. However, since all senses are attributes of the natural man and contribute to the quality of one's life on earth, they will be completed and will add to the infinite happiness in heaven.

Also, what is true of the external senses is true of the internal or emotional senses. We speak of these more often as sensibilities, the sources of passion and emotion which can increase or diminish according to the slightest shifting of one's attitude. Thus a sense of love, as one's love of beautiful things, seems to be the source of all other passions of delight — desire, joy, anticipation, boldness, as well as the human failings of fear, despair, and anger. But in heaven these will operate only on the side of pleasure. There will be no sense of fear, aversion, or apprehension once desire is fulfilled and the good is completely possessed. Hope will completely overthrow despair or the irascible need to strive for what is desired. All hypersensitivity or recognition of deprivation must give way before fulfillment. At the same time there will be the immediate union or harmony between the reception of stimuli and sensual pleasure and sensation. Also, unless we are ready for and attuned to the infinite our hope of attaining heaven will be lessened even here on earth. We must be confident that the ultimate of our hope not only may be anticipated but will be realized.

For some people there may be a feeling of disappointment about heaven in the idea that once they arrive, and are there body and soul, it will be a dull attainment — the frightening thought may occur that "there won't be anything to do!" Some may even think that in this "state of being" they will have nothing to do but stand about like sightseers looking up at magnificent scenery, gaping goggle-eyed at things they will understand but will be obliged to look at again and again forever. Not in the least. First, infinity requires the utmost variety and diversity. Second, in heaven the body and soul which constitute the complete human creature will perform every act of the mind and body which are necessary and in accord with its created purpose. And since motion (or agility) is natural to man, it will not be denied anyone. Being limited to a static condition would be to impose restriction and this again is a penalty which cannot be thought of in heaven.

The glorified body will not only be agile and move freely, but also it will have the power of subtlety. Agility means the power or ability to transport oneself from one place, one set of circumstances, to another with the rapidity of thought. Subtlety means that glorified bodies will be given the capability of penetrating the hardest of substances, to pass through rather than go around — and that no obstacle can be placed in the way of movement. This may be likened to the rays of the sun penetrating a clear crystal. Agility and subtlety might be likened to electricity which travels along a wire. Electricity does not displace the wire or change the wire to effect its passage, yet the movement is almost instantaneous. This also is made clearer by our new and greater understanding of molecular compenetrability. These attributes are some of those possessed by a spiritual body, they are the natural properties of spirits. And these are bestowed as rewards upon the glorified body of the human person.

In heaven you will not have to walk a mile for pleasure. Freedom of movement means that there will be no obstacles to hinder movement, and there will be no attendant effort, no muscle strain, no struggle to go up hill or down. It means that wherever you wish to go in heaven or God's universe you will be able to move there without exertion — and without the pain of disappointment upon arrival.

Spiritual or glorified bodies are like this for they have been given qualities which are theirs as a necessary condition. We can derive some further idea of this from the scientific knowledge that all matter is made up of infinitely small particles called atoms, mesons, etc., and these in turn have other even smaller units within them. A spiritualized body might be likened to one which would have control, at will, of the energy resting in and about these particles. For instance, a spiritual body can go through a door without opening it and be immediately, without a lapse of time, where it wishes to be. In heaven, there will be no restraining or confining partitions, no straight-jacket rules, to hamper motion. If there were, it would mean restriction, in degree, and restriction is limitation, and limitation is measurement, and measurement requires time, and with time there simply would be no heaven.

Because this is all beyond our human experience, beyond dreaming almost, it appears as fantastic, jolly fun. It will be. There is only one word to describe it, a word that keeps popping up even among the most intelligent of those who attempt to write about heaven. That word is *ineffable*, which means something that cannot be expressed; something for which we have no experiential background and no vocabulary competence to speak or write of it. So far as happiness is concerned, and this is the total of our heavenly experience in anticipation now and in actuality later in heaven, your joy will be ineffable!

VII

Through love to light! O wonderful the way
That leads from darkness to the perfect day!
— R.W. Gilder, *After-song.*

As a fruitless but intriguing pastime it is interesting and natural to speculate about who will be in heaven. Many people look around on earth and consider that heaven is going to provide their revenge upon others. Their attitude is, "Whoopee, I'm going to heaven, and I'm damned certain you're not!" Heaven is going to be, they think, the place where they will "get even" with their more fortunate neighbors who possess more of this world's compounders of headaches. For them heaven will be where "November has its revenge upon May" once and for always.

These people are just a step ahead of another group who feel that heaven will be the means of compensating themselves, of perpetually satisfying their natural avarice, of supplying them with the car or fur coat and jewels they covet now.

This "pie in the sky" idea that some people come to assume as the ultimate in heaven is the result of flawed human nature seeking vengeance on enemies and compensation for what is lacking on earth. If we look at heaven from this low viewpoint and try to make it a warehouse of artifacts, knick-knacks, and boondoggled objects of earth, we will remain in the dark, seeing only darkly. And as long as we consider what the Joneses have and the Smiths lack as a gauge for one's participation in heaven, we get further away from any idea about who will be in heaven. Instead it is our right desire, in fact a serious part of our own goal, that all people should be in heaven since that is the will of the Creator.

There are many people who each one of us thinks should not be in heaven. And some would keep out each one of us for some reason or other. Selfishness does not make a good judge when drawing up a list of the socially acceptable for heaven, nor does a too lenient attitude. What we are all aware of is simple — not everyone is going to be in heaven. We each can say during life that we will make the music and dance to the tune as we travel through life. But our hope is that finally the instruments that we are, will be in tune and complete before we waltz into that undiscovered country. We are aware, every day of our lives, that our cradle stands in the grave, but that only death will supply our final leap of exhilaration.

Each one of us knows that the beautiful answer is always for the one who asks a beautiful question, so we keep asking ourselves again and again that question of finality according to our own experience of truth. Andre Maurois said, "There are certain persons for whom pure truth is a prison." But finality is not easier to face even when we beguile ourselves into thinking "we've got it made." One thing is certain, as the Bible tells us, we should look forward to glory and not back to failure. In the patient reality of all living things we must come to realize that with death "worms are the words, but joy is the voice," as e.e. cummings said.

Everyone knows that there are people with whom they would not like to share heaven. Who would want to spend an eternity with some of the creeps of human history, some of the hideous monsters that have traversed the span of life. And we must be aware that the quality of life is not judged by the distance traveled but by the road taken.

Of course, everyone knows that the saints are in heaven and thinks it is only right. Who would have it otherwise? The friends who love the most should surely be with their God who is Love. We are happy that they are there. It gives us assurance in our hope. But besides these beatified ones, who are the other people in the "mighty multitude," the eight groups St. John writes of metaphorically in the Book of Revelation? To say that their name is legion is too distant a view, like looking at people in a parade from the top of the Empire State Building. We can neither see them as individuals nor count them. Yet, even in speculation we cannot point a finger at this man with a reputation for good judgment and that lady who is always ready to serve others and say they will be in heaven. Just who, then, will be in heaven? We cannot judge.

Most fortunately for us, we do not have the burden of judging who will be in heaven and who will not. Suffice it to say there will be a great, great number of people. Heaven's computers are not limited. Surely, there will be a perfectly sufficient number. Does that mean in hopeful reckoning that every human person will be there? Not at all. Who are we kidding? Who thinks that every acorn that falls grows into an oak tree? Those in heaven will be those who are willing to make the trip, or to put it another way and bring the "willing" into focus, all those who learn the Way and follow Him — all who have the will to desire God and the love to fulfill desire. We might adapt the patriotic speech of Patrick Henry in addressing the Virginia Convention when he affirmed: "We are not weak if we make a proper use of those means which the God of nature has placed in our power ... The battle, sir, is not to the strong alone, it is to the vigilant, the active, the brave." Verily the goal for Christians and all who seek the true God is not reached by the weak of spirit but by the heroic good. After scaling the mountains of life, we all will look down the long savannah of our fulfilled expectations and there we shall find the very font of peace.

In fact, it might seem easier to speculate on who will not be in heaven. But here again, we are apt to be influenced by human vengefulness, petty eyebrow-raising, a finger-pointing type of judging. The best we can do is make wild conjectures, but leave plenty of room for surprise and human error — for our human computers are faulty when we try to assess quality and numbers in our emotional and wishful way of thinking. Contrary to common misconceptions, in heaven there will be sinners, prostitutes, criminals, and enemies. There will be thieves, like Dismas of the Bible (Lk. 23:40-43), and as for enemies, it can be said that the degree of their enmity is not always the measure of their individual guilt.

One thing can be said definitely: the thieves, prostitutes, personal and social enemies will not be in heaven because of their thievery, prostitution, or enmity. It will not matter how proficient or expert people were in their professions either. We know of many others whose lifestyles make them neither more likely candidates nor assure them of even a minor place among the blessed. It is a fact that no members of nation, profession, or religion will be in heaven simply because of their membership in that group on earth. No one has a corner on heaven whether first banana in the revue or last lady in the chorus line. So don't become a plumber or candlestick maker or even a monk or a mother or a civil rights worker, thinking that the occupation has a guarantee to heaven written into your papers of apprenticeship. The expertise is needed not in life's occupation but in the living of life itself.

No condition of human nature will be a determining factor in heaven. There will be black people, yellow people, red, and white people, as well as all the admixture of colors in between. But they will not be there *because* of color. Nor will men, women, or children be there *because* of race or their social standing, or *because* they won honors from universities or received pontifical or national medals. The soldier won't be there because of soldiering or the farmer because of his husbandry. Not all priests, or ministers or rabbis or bishops or cardinals or presidents or girls who are titled "Miss Universe" of any year will be there simply because of their office or honor or dignity or lack of it. In short, no vocation, no sphere of activity nor any attribute of human existence of itself is any guarantee of getting into heaven or being left out of it.

It may seem that this has been stressed too much, this qualification list or the "select" sheet, but it is a basic mistake of those who fear they may have less or more of a chance to go to heaven than so-and-so who drives a Lincoln and wears alligator shoes. And don't worry, there will be ample room for all. You alone are responsible for your reservation. No crowding, no pushing, no jockeying for position or queuing up — and the last one in will not even have to close the door. Entrance is "soully" the result of "higher" living, or as St. Paul says, "Seek the things that are higher" (Col. 3:1ff.).

Being in heaven is strictly an individual affair. You book passage for yourself and you make the trip alone, as an individual. You can use whatever tour director you wish, select what means of travel suits you best. But you arrive alone. And once there, you are an individual, not a member of any group, not a guest or merely a joiner along for the ride, but a perfected individual. There may be some on earth who aided you, helped you pack for the trip, so to speak, but their aid is more their joy than yours in the end.

Don't misunderstand us when we say you will be alone in heaven. Not alone in the sense of no one else being there, for there must be a social aspect of heaven since human persons are sociable by nature.

Indeed there will be plenty of others; but you will be alone, uniquely alone, as far as your personal joy, your glory and participation are concerned. You will be in one place where you alone can be and to which no other person can aspire or attain as reward. This means there will be no sharing or division of what is yours by attainment or by merit because that would be a limitation — and such would destroy the joy itself since division is impossible to that wonderful oneness of being with God.

All of this does not mean that you are going to be apart from other persons, or kept in solitary or isolation, enjoying only your own complete satisfaction. You will be able to see others, enjoy their company and witness their joy — and this will be an added joy for you. This we know because an expression of love of neighbor is, even in nature, a manifestation of our love of God. Our neighbor on earth perchance is unloving toward us, may even ignore us. And we might have to admit that even here the difficulties, unpleasantness, sometimes arise not from our neighbor but from ourselves who are too selfish to love. No, the gregarious nature of humans, their propensity for social contacts, since all will be perfected, will provide each person with friendship and the amiable companionship of others in heaven.

We can take a closer look at this idea: "If I'm to be alone, how can I be with others?" Well, you won't be identified with them or be classified with them as part of a crowd. You will be alone in the possession and perfect enjoyment of heaven as yourself. Put it this way: a group of tourists look out over the Grand Canyon, each person looking at the same objects, the wonderful play of colors, the variety, but each one enjoys the view in his or her own way, as only each one can enjoy it. No two people standing there are filled with the same awe, the same feeling of beauty and grandeur. And each sightseer derives joy from the same view in a different degree. This is true in the physical order of things as well as in different mental appreciations, for one may be partly colorblind and miss the purple haze. Another might have more sensitive hearing and be able to catch the murmur of water far below or a bird's song in flight, but each can feel wonder and in no way can either be said to "share" in the beauty.

In this each person is alone, as in heaven each is alone in his own perfection and degree of union with God. As St. Augustine says,

"Oh, happy I and thrice happy, if, after the dissolution of the body, I shall merit to hear the songs that are sung in praise of the Eternal King, by the inhabitants of the celestial city!"

The distinction, which will prescind from this unique aloneness and add to each individual's joy in singular ways is made by merit. We understand that each person comes to heaven with the assurance of obtaining the prize which he or she has won. The Psalmist declares: "One thing God said; these two things which I heard: that power belongs to God, and yours, O Lord, is kindness; and that you render to everyone according to his deeds" (Ps. 62:12). Each service receives its own reward — yet we are too humble to dare speak of our own merits. But we comprehend that where a reward is promised we have a right in justice to receive that which is ours alone.

VIII

With this broad knowledge of who will be in heaven and how each will be uniquely alone in his or her enjoyment, we now draw near to the many additional joys of heaven which may be called the social delights. These are the "specials" which will be granted to everyone over and above individual perfection. Social blessings will not be the result of a celestial caste system nor a glorified democracy with strong emphasis upon equality. Such earthly ideas, such utopian efforts or processes whereby every created being is declared equal in accordance with some new scale of values, are not true of heaven. We have already disposed of that idea by describing the unique, individual participation in heaven. There is a big word for it that simply means "considering man's ultimate end there is no equality," or *teleologically* all persons are not equal, that is, as to position in heaven. But the social joys of heaven are supreme and perfect delights that will be enjoyed by everyone. These are much like the joys that we envision on earth as we strive with a multitude of government systems, all of which have failed to reach the absolute ideal up to the present time in history.

All humans love the society of others. But on earth there are some dangers associated with the too-close association of peoples. Some are threats to others because of feelings of insecurity. Some persons with even the best intentions betray our love and cause us sorrow. These are imperfections with which our earthly life is confronted daily. Jealousy, envy, selfish and thoughtless actions will always be a part of our existence because of personality defects and just plain human orneriness. To console his daughter Margaret, St. Thomas More said, "We shall all meet merrily in heaven." This is not empty promise but a positive joy to look forward to ... the reunion of friends and all joined in love with Love. We read in the Bible: "So then you are no longer strangers and sojourners, but you are fellow citizens with the holy ones and members of the household of God" (Eph. 2:19).

The first of the five social joys will be *equality of virtue* on the part of everyone in heaven. This might be described as a certain transcendent quality of goodness which will not be given to a person according to his or her individual place in heaven but which will be possessed simply because of each person's presence there. Even on earth we can realize that this would be a great boon to everyone. Just think, no villains, no depraved characters, no self-seekers to cause pain and trouble. And is it not true that it is the unvirtuous people who cause you the most sorrow here on earth? No matter how beautiful, how charming or otherwise endowed a person may be, if he or she is a genuine "stinker," a graduate of the obnoxious school, we are repulsed. Association with such a person is not only not a blessing, but a downright pain in the neck. The very fact that "the millwheels of desire are turned by the rivers of pain" in this life should only convince us the more of the genuine joys of being virtuous and being in a virtuous company in the hereafter.

Simply circulating in heaven must be a really tremendous joy. Imagine knowing that every smile is one hundred percent sincere, every movement interpreted justly, every word truthful, and every instance of interaction free from the pettiness that mars so many of our social contacts on earth. There will be nothing to annoy, irritate, or rub one the wrong way — and nothing to make a person repulsive to others. The ultimate in perfect, good fellowship will be found everywhere and enjoyed by all — it's an added joy which can be measured only by the limits of our desire for such society here on earth.

The second social joy is the perfect equality which is sustained by the *equal learning* of those in heaven. As Aldous Huxley says, "Knowledge is always a function of being." This means that in heaven, since intelligence is the greatest capability of humans, all will have an equally extensive grasp of knowledge and truth. This does not mean the individual's participation in the infinite wisdom of God, for this will be according to the degree of the individual's perfection through grace and merit. Rather, this equality means the mental endowment that will be the perfection of the human mind, the ability to grasp a truth and appreciate its wonder, or the mental capability to know.

On earth we are constantly striving to attain a greater spread of education to bring every person's store of knowledge to a condition of harmony. We build schools, universities, special institutes, and wind up with professors squabbling with associate professors, and wise-guys contradicting specialists. This we say is mere perversity. And we have few and only fleeting moments when great minds do meet in accord and indulge the pleasures of sharing some understanding of the beauty and simplicity of truth. A genuine consensus even of opinions is humanly very difficult to arrive at as anyone knows who has ever sat on a committee or ventured into the political arena. The person who has found a smidgeon of truth through his life's experience or the trial and error of the work syndrome knows that the resulting pleasure is a hard won and brief satisfaction.

But as an essential consequence of being in heaven, with this immediate learning we will be able to share in, for example, the majesty of perfect music, insights beyond our acquired knowledge, and our aptitude for "appreciation and appeal" so that we will relish all the arts through heightened cultural awareness.

The third social joy of those in heaven is one which is first experienced on earth as a genuine pleasure. In heaven it will be perfected and everyone will possess this as an attribute — everlastingly present in an unchanging condition. It is none other than *personal beauty*. Each one in heaven will have his or her own distinctively perfect beauty. This will be not only beauty of body, but it will be a unique radiance — an effulgence that each will have as part of individual perfection. We will be able to recognize each person easily for it will create about each one an aura which is distinct and recognizable. Artists throughout the ages have attempted to show this holy aura by painting halos and aureoles about the images of saints — an idea originating with the biblical description of the Transfiguration of Christ.

To put this another way, the human person may be likened now to a light bulb which has form when unlit, but which when lighted has both form and radiance. So it is with persons in heaven, each shall be seen surrounded by his or her own special splendor. Similarly, some have thought of the union of body and soul as a candle's wick dipped in wax and both ends burning with intense light.

On earth, deformity and ugliness repel, while beauty attracts. In heaven also, we will derive pleasure from looking upon beauty. It does not mean a special superficial style of beauty, a fashion or type, such as that repeatedly provided by common fad on earth — the upswept, the hungdown, or the wrung-out. No, this means perfect beauty of body, the symmetry, the balance, the proportion which each person as an individual is blessed with as his or her own singular share in the essence of true beauty. It means perfection and harmony in the glorified body and reflections of unalloyed beauty that will radiate from the body and give joy. Each of us will become one of heaven's "beautiful people."

Even now we sometimes see the foreshadowing of such beauty in a smile, or in the face of a mother looking at her child, or in great character seen in the faces of truly outstanding men and women. The personal beauty of each person in heaven will be all of these and infinitely more — and each one will be in degree a reflection of the infinite beauty of God. Such beauty will be in both the beholder and in the possessor. As such it will be an added joy to each soul observing this beauty in himself and in those others who participate in the bliss of heaven. As Kahlil Gibran says in his book *The Prophet*: " ... beauty is not a need but an ecstasy ... beauty is eternity gazing at itself in a mirror. But you are eternity and you are the mirror."

For the pleasure of companionship there is required an additional quality which forms our fourth social joy in heaven. This additional lineament, possessed by everyone in heaven, is *refinement* — a certain distinct hallmark of real nobility. Now, do not mistake us. This does not mean the mere following of manners or prescribed conventions such as the Amy Vanderbilt ideal of good manners, which is merely conventional courtesy — and surely not the way to be a "thoroughbred." These are only standards which help to assure a degree of good behavior toward others, where charity may be wanting, and to keep our earthly social contacts from resulting in mayhem or at least disorder. Have you ever noticed that the klutzy, boorish, ill-mannered, and obnoxious human person usually causes us more disquietude, more distaste and uneasiness than does the cultivated and very smooth individual?

It must be admitted that even here on earth the marks of refinement or distinction are admired as adornments which somehow add to personal beauty. The crude or loutish are scorned and shunned, while the person having even a small amount of "polish" seems to take on an added attractiveness. Having some degree of good manners enables one to impress and please without the usual amount of bodily beauty. One's personality is always enhanced by refined appearance and good taste. The coarse, the ill-mannered, the oaf, the cad, anyone lacking in compassion or sensitivity, repels rather than attracts, engenders disgust rather than pleasure.

It is thoroughly reasonable common sense to declare that in heaven, where our entire nature is perfected together with learning being increased for the mind and physical beauty for the body, there will be an elegance added whereby each will appear to others with complete attractiveness. Were this not so, it would be impossible to associate with everyone in heaven — not out of any idea of snobbery, but because the perfect would be repelled by the imperfect, which is an impossibility there.

This refinement in heaven will be part of both the mind and the heart, a quality which will make one completely "loveable," that gives one the true romance of being fully and perfectly noble. And this will add infinitely to our social pleasures in heaven, even as on earth we are all pleased to associate with truly enlightened and cultivated persons who are gracious in their bearing and in their response to our affection and esteem.

It could not be otherwise in our enjoyment of heaven and in the enjoyment of those other persons who will be present. For each one will reflect in degree that glorious goodness which is found to an infinite extent in God. As Dante declared: "Like the lark that soars in the air, first singing, then silent, content with the last sweetness that satiates it, such seemed to me that image, the imprint of the Eternal Pleasure" (Par. XX, 73).

The perfect possession of these first four social pleasures in heaven virtue, learning, personal beauty, and refinement — make necessary the fifth social joy which is *mutual love* or true *charity*. This is without any doubt the very center, the very heart of heaven. God is Love, and seeing Him as He is, we shall have this perfect love for Him as He has love for each of us. Alvarez de Pas, writing of prayer, hints of this "nearness to love," saying: "The soul sees herself *near* God; she sees herself loved and esteemed, the object of a special providence, like a very dear daughter ... The soul understands, as it were experimentally, that which she only knew before by faith namely, that she is seen of God, tenderly loved by Him; quite near to Him who is prompt to benefit her, and grant her desires." This love of God for us is reflective in that we can see it and share in it among others in heaven.

Because persons in heaven see one another in God, they and the saints love one another. This could not be otherwise since all are *near* to God. Each one rejoices in the degree of blessedness which others have received, and each will love the other, for this belongs to essential beatitude. You all have experienced here on earth a feeling of joy, of satisfaction and completeness, when you see a friend or a neighbor who is happy. There is a sharing in happiness which adds to the showing of love for one another. The selfish, the niggardly have difficulty in sharing happiness. But not so the persons in heaven whose association with others will produce new joys and compound them. Take away enemies, remove those who seek to cause harm, and you have extended the social love which will be everyone's in heaven.

We will experience in heaven the depth and the fullness of love with no lessening, no reverse, no holding back, and no ending. This love will have the ultimate of joy because it will have no loss, no boredom, no farewells. As perfect love it will not suffer the "little deaths that partings are." Love will be love without pain — or the fear of losing the love of someone, for loss of human love is pain suffered only on earth.

In heaven, everyone will be loved by everyone else. Love will be given and returned perfectly — because each will share in the infinite love of God who is all Love. This is hard to understand because we must consider it with our human limitations, in the context of our experience of love on earth. There will be no enemy or anyone who contradicts love, no detractor, no one to criticize, belittle, misjudge, or gossip. Our love for others in heaven will be complete and perfect sharing, as we share the divine Good. Our love will have many delights which will be like the act — impossible on earth — of lifting a smile, with all of its goodness and beauty, from a loved one's face to treasure its perfection for all eternity. In heaven, unlike earth, our relationship with God will be real and strong beyond our dreams and, with our fellow participants, it will be both close and wonderful.

The five social joys of heaven will bring about a perfect get-together. It will be more than a grand party because everyone will be host or hostess and at the same instance, guest. We can make no sure comparisons here, but we know that when joy is expanded to infinity and all powers to enjoy are so broadened, there is an added fillip, a greater extension of enjoyment. And in heaven you won't have to write home about it, or send up a shout — everyone there will know it and be perfectly happy because you are perfectly happy in fulfillment and in sharing.

Through consideration of these many social joys we arrive at two conditions which make heaven a real place of glamour-glory. These will fill our souls with the ultimate of all our desires. They will satisfy all our senses and sensibilities to repletion and saturation but without blinding us, deafening us, or giving us that overstuffed feeling. They will be essential conditions wherein one's glorified body and soul will revel. They will surround our entire being with a resplendent effulgence which is infinitely brighter than having all the spotlights of the world turned upon us. They will add to and complete the society we enjoy. What we have already considered, together with the ineffable presence of God, are not all of beatitude. These, it is true, are wonderful beyond imagination and perfectly delightful, but we need still other conditions to bring us to a full awareness of all these many blessings. This may be difficult, but let's push our reason just a little further.

Heaven might be said to have an *atmosphere*, a quality which pervades the existence of those participating in its glory.

This quality, this ineffable ambiance, is made up of some of the most choice rewards of heaven itself.

The first of these essentials is *tranquillity* or *peace*. St. Augustine has said that peace is the "tranquillity of order." We can examine and understand something about this quality in the light of our earthly experience. We hear much about peace lately — personal peace, national peace, international peace, peace here and peace there. It is the desirable good of the moment, the most sought after goal of today's people. But the peace we visualize here on earth is only the absence of contention; and a time of great oppression may, in these terms, be a time of peace. The peace of heaven is much more. We may suppose it is exactly that quality which Christ spoke of when He greeted the apostles after His resurrection with the words, "Peace be to you!" Certainly the apostles were not fighting, but afraid, and even this peace could not remain with them as they witnessed to the truth. Wherever there is mission there is struggle — and when there is struggle peace may not be present in the complete sense.

On earth we do know moments of peace; we enjoy at times some degree of rest or at least a temporary cessation of effort. At other times, and more frequently for some, there are gratifications for the mind, times when we feel the exaltation of accomplishment or discovery of some magnificence or truth. There are vast compensations that give genuine joy at the overcoming of obstacles, yet even they lack the final good they will possess in heaven. This final quality which raises every pleasure of heaven to the nth plus degree and sustains it at this incredible intensity is the simple truth that in heaven perfect enjoyment will be in a context of true peace — enjoyment forever which will never change. This *unchangableness* is at the center of such peace.

The peace of heaven is not "peace of soul" about which we have read, and which is spoken of as though it were a balm put on one's original wound — (the wound which Adam and all his descendants have been contending with all these centuries). Nor is the peace of heaven to be thought of as the peace of mind that is regarded as a kind of poultice to cure and guard against future attacks of anxiety. These are borrowings of the word "peace" and hold out only temporary means of putting us at ease in life which is a great and interesting struggle, wherein we fight for peace but cannot hope to possess it while the fight continues. What should be intended in the use of "peace" in these human terms is that peace is not attained by giving up the struggle or fleeing from the strife but rather by having patience while the fight of life continues. Everyone can learn to strive for heaven where true peace is to be had, for — "by your perseverance you will secure your lives" (Lk. 21:19).

The peace we desire is that which can free us from outside forces that would shape us according to their way and against what we really want in life. This peace is like a prayer — its reward is both in what is prayed for and in the very act of praying itself. It is reflective, turning back toward ourselves, giving peace in the very receiving of it. Dante declared in his *Paradiso* that "in God's will is our peace." We have in heaven the promised fulfillment. We shall not have to do daily combat there for what we will have in infinite abundance.

The peace of heaven is, of course, order, perfect harmony. It brings its own rapture. And it does so primarily because there is nothing to disturb or destroy. There is no conflict, no contending for an object to satisfy a desire, no dissension or clash of wills with a neighbor, no currying of favor, no squabbling over who is to receive the five or ten percent to assure some monetary good. It is more, for it is also freedom from worry about the past or future. In this peace there is no memory of the past to sadden or haunt us, and no foreboding of the unexpected or unknown of the future. There is no brooding about what will be, because it simply *is*.

We will have peace with ourselves, in our minds and souls. No restless, nagging hopes and fears which beset our daily routine now. On earth, this kind of peace can never be attained. We may be riding along smoothly, everything being in what we call "apple-pie order." But suddenly, a tire blows out and we discover the softness of the road's shoulder is not soft at all. In heaven there will be no sudden jolting, no disquieting, bone-crushing, crippling surprises. There is secure harmony, perfect balance, and proportion. It is this that makes possible the enjoyment of the delights of heaven, for without harmony doubts would arise and no doubt or unanswered question can be a part of heaven.

We realize this peace is that which St. Paul spoke of to the first Philippians and which once fulfilled can never be lessened. He prayed: "Then the peace of God that surpasses all understanding will guard your hearts and minds in Christ Jesus" (Phil. 4:7).

Besides peace, there is the second essential which is allied to peace and yet is distinct from it. This quality might be called *rest* or the absence of struggle or arduous effort. It is the rest which St. John recorded in the Book of Revelation, saying, " 'Yes,' said the Spirit, 'let them find rest from their labors, for their good works accompany them!' " (Rev. 14:13). It is the consolation of accomplishment — the rest that was God's after the major acts of creation (Gen. 2:2). While the rest of the blessed is ineffable, it is yet operative and somehow ever active.

Here on earth we constantly make efforts, flexing those muscles, beating those brains, walking that mile. Tiredness is the toll of toil. Even the seekers of the "fast buck" become weary just holding out their hands. In playing the slot machine of life the handle becomes more and more difficult to pull even for the smallest payoffs. And what of the "credit slaves" who with fixed bayonets are always rushing at the carrying charge, the fixed price index, the inflation that grows on nothingness. You think this is an easy, comfortable living? It is life's irony that we keep struggling with or for something and continue to wrestle with fatigue, weariness, or disgust when we have attained a goal that is temporary. There is never any genuine consolation, nor is the race always won by the strong. The very pursuit of earthly rest sometimes has its own wage — sleepless, restless nights. In heaven, the toil is ended, no more disheartening struggle and not even the boredom of unpacking after the weariness of our life's journey.

What a consolation, what a reward, this "eternal rest"! Yet rest in heaven is not going to be like a long sleep. It will not be utter collapse, a suspension of activity, a turning of the mind to butter that ends up in endless doodling or cutting out paper dolls. On the contrary, it will be complete activity with full play of all the energies of body and mind — without any of the consequences we endure on earth. It will be activity like the constant movement of the wind, motion without exertion, progress in the perpetual act of accomplishment — the pleasure of bodily motion and thought.

This rest will include the enjoyment of one's exercise of the mind in contemplating truths the mind was intended to seek as rational pleasure. To know without having to study or learn, to comprehend without the tedium of life's constant searching for even a grain of knowledge, this is a part of heavenly rest. It means repose in glory, with constant attainment — not the reaching out of the hand, but the continuous grasping of the good and holding it without effort, without tiring of possessing it. What'll you have? — You will have it.

We mentioned before the enjoyment of the faculties of the soul. We touched on enjoyment through intellect, the highest faculty of our being. Now consider that in the life in heaven an *intellectual pleasure* is joined to the joy of peace and rest. This might be called the perfect exercise of the mind, the pleasure that arises from the mind's grasp of knowledge — the joy of knowing and total understanding.

In heaven, the mind has its true joy in wisdom. If on earth men will struggle, go without sleep, lose their health, give up natural pleasures to pursue knowledge, it must have its own joy. In heaven this joy is forever compounded, free of doubt or chance of error — and with beauty of expression, of having and also sharing wisdom. It is a pleasure that is exquisite, of the highest order. It is a sharing in the secrets of the universe and a perpetual insight into the truth which is God and God's way with all created good. If the astronaut and the astronomer marvel at the magnitude and magnificence of creation, then what will be everyone's joy at knowing the truth and the infinite wonders of the universe?

If the rule were given that heaven was to be enjoyed for only a limited time, there would still be the urge, the imperative to go there, to see and know the undiscovered country. Its joy so great would still afford the strongest attraction. However, we know it cannot end, for a limit of duration placed upon it would be a sadness, and would rob its every joy of some pleasure. It would then be a penalty and an injustice of which God is incapable. Besides, we know, if we know anything, that heaven has been declared to be "everlasting," which means it will never cease. This we know from the Bible, from our innermost thoughts, from our self-assurance that this hour, this grain of sand, cannot be the end-all and be-all of our existence.

Everlastingness is our ultimate bonanza. On earth the sunset fades, the beauty of nature corrodes or erodes, man's wrought beauty palls, and the beloved dies. But in heaven peace continues, rest endures, love is forever the triumph of possession, and the truth is immutable. The senses revel without sating themselves, the mind finds and possesses and cherishes, the body absorbs and reflects the light of its glory. Forever, in heaven, is not just a long time. To put it as simply and obscurely as words can, forever is being forever.

IX

God is more truly imagined than expressed,
and He exists more truly than imagined.
— St. Augustine, *De Trinitate.*

One truth is ever uppermost in our thinking. We each know this as surely as we know the way of our coming and going through a doorway. This fact is that all life on earth comes to an end. The ultimate irresponsibility, the real madness of human living happens when one attempts denial of this truth. And why should we? Don't we look about us, observe and count the hours even as we strew them into the winds that buffet our lives?

For some, the fact of death is a sadness they cannot face, even in their final moments. Why? The opening and closing of a door is not sadness. Christ said, "I am the door," and entry comes easily if we have lived in recognition of the presence of the door. Perhaps what bothers most of us is the brevity of life. Those who have plenty of the material goods of the world tell themselves they have everything they want, they are content and wish for this condition to continue on and on, despite the known truth that it must end. They are hard pressed to accept the truth of living — which is that living eventually stops. But even they know that the spiritual surpasses the material in value and in duration, just as the glory that comes to everyone who attains the spiritual far transcends the fleeting glitter of the material kingdom.

Let us put it in a simple manner. We have learned that the lives we lead are anchored in love, through hope. And what expresses love better than service — "whoever wishes to be great among you shall be your servant; whoever wishes to be first among you shall be your slaves," Christ tells us (Mt. 20:26-27). Serving them will teach us eventually to respond with love to Love when we come to death. This love leads us from self-isolation into a living, joyous communion with one's fellow human beings. For loving transforms us, as St. Paul wrote: "All of us, gazing with unveiled face on the glory of the Lord, are being transformed into the same image from glory to glory, as from the Lord who is the Spirit" (2 Cor. 3:18).

We have touched upon this quality of love before. When we think of death — the transition, the opening of the door, the transformation — we should have no feeling of sadness. We know we are part of a greater, more comprehensive plan. "Divinity is not playful. The universe was not made in jest but in solemn incomprehensible earnest," says Annie Dillard, "not as she who looks upon life as a trip up and down the landscape of this ... brief day."

Likewise in the promise we have been given there is a consolation beyond any other, beyond any possible reward of material things. Isaiah declares it, speaking God's words: "Because you are precious in my eyes and honored, and I love you, I give men in return for you, peoples in exchange for your life. Fear not, for I am with you; I will bring your offspring from the east, and from the west I will gather you; I will say to the north, Give up, and to the south, Do not withhold; bring my sons from afar and my daughters from the end of the earth, every one who is called by my name, whom I created for my glory, whom I formed and made. Bring forth the people who are blind, yet have eyes, who are deaf, yet have ears! Let all the nations gather together and let the peoples assemble. Who among them can declare this, and show us the former things? Let them bring their witnesses to justify them, and let them hear and say, It is true. 'You are my witnesses,' says the LORD, and my servant whom I have chosen, that you may know and believe me and understand that I am He. Before me no god was formed, nor shall there be any after me....

"Thus says the LORD, the King of Israel and his Redeemer, the LORD of hosts: 'I am the first and I am the last; besides me there is no god. (cf. Rev. 22:12-14) Who is like me? Let him proclaim it, let him declare and set it forth before me. Who has announced from of old the things to come? Let them tell us what is yet to be. Fear not, nor be afraid; have I not told you from of old and declared it? And you are my witnesses! Is there a God besides me?' " (Is. 43:4-10; 44:6-8 — Revised Standard Version, Thomas Nelson & Sons, Ltd.).

After life is the time for reaping. The harvest comes with a bounty which none of us can ever assess. Our best guesstimate would be not even a poor approximation. What we do know is that the transition from the present to the future, to the life hereafter, is swift as breath. In the Book of Wisdom we read of this swift change: ''All those things have vanished like a shadow, and like a rumor that passes by; like a ship that sails through the billowy water, and when it has passed no trace can be found, nor track of its keel in the waves; or as, when a bird flies through the air, no evidence of its passage is found; the light air, lashed by the beat of its pinions and pierced by the force of its rushing flight, is traversed by the movement of its wings, and afterward no sign of its coming is found there; or as, when an arrow is shot at a target, the air, thus divided, comes together at once, so that no one knows its pathway'' (Wis. 5:9-12).

We quickly live and quickly go into the bright hope where all is reward and all is related to this life's living as daylight is to dawn. In hope there is no fear, for the promise of hope is in the living of one's life, just as yeast is in the bread to give it fullness and flavor.

Though we will walk in the "valley of death" there is no fear, but a great joy in what is to come. It is the ultimate truth, the incomprehensible truth, that we do not go to the "kingdom" but that the "kingdom" comes to us. We are not the seeker, we are the quarry, we are the sought; we are not the lost, we are the found. God and man are on a journey toward each other.

Our thinking about heaven has been flawed on many counts over the past years. Stories became beliefs, dreams became nightmares of mingled fears and wild hopes. For us the legends seem a means of learning which we have come to accept more or less as fact. In human terms we have been taught the myth of heaven, the three-storied accounts we have become accustomed to hearing and reading. These presented a kind of sandwich effect: heaven above, hell below and earth between. The variations were only what imagination could supply and they all limped badly, ranging from the circles of Dante to "Green Pastures," from the River Styx to the "pearly gates." All this must be changed in our thinking. It is not fitting for rational man to accept these mythologized accounts symbolically in light of the many new discoveries in our world and our universe.

Of course we cannot finalize our thoughts, but as the culmination of our present thinking there are several further, real areas of speculation that we can pursue with some degree of satisfaction. These in no way will change the "delight of faith" which we are assured is ours. Instead they will broaden our viewpoint as we attempt to encompass some of the many insights we have gained from recent scientific excursions.

This all means that we move beyond the overly simple idea of hell as a place of sensual pain and heaven as a place of sensual delight. We can search and find intelligible meaning which satisfies us, not within the imagined topology of heaven but within our limited human reason. It is in this way that we recognize the myths of future life and accept the story for what it is. We can view the biblical translations and literary devices of many authors and accept their meaning without being zapped by their literal descriptions and often outlandish imaginings. For we, as all believing Christians, know by *faith*, not merely because of narrative accounts, of the resurrection and the reward of everlasting life. And we reject such fripperies as reincarnation, transmigration of spirits, and various types of nirvana.

How does all this affect our reasonable thinking in the attempt to understand heaven? It is first necessary to endeavor to locate God in a space-time manner of expression — to give Him place and a reference area in our "calendar of events," in our own time slot. But we also must realize that becoming too specific — trying to say "here and now" — is too destructive of the myth we have learned and come to accept as an appealing concept, one which we in our limitations can understand. We cannot change God who is immutable, ever unchanging, even in our consciousness, and in our personal faith wherein we view God in a most singular manner. Secondly, by loving speculation, we will not in any way weaken or endanger our faith, but rather strengthen it to our great benefit. We can think about the quality of heaven, that is, its freedom from hatred, envy, and all the other conditions which now tempt us and weaken us, humanly speaking. Heaven, we know, must be free of these.

There are other pleasant speculations which add to heaven's attractions. First to be considered is our concern for people we have known and loved here on earth. What of the many friends, relatives, and other people who fill our earthly lives, sometimes with an abundance of love and joy, and at other times with sadness and disappointment? One thing we can say surely is that there will be no sadness, no consciousness of pain because that would be a negation of the essential joy of heaven. At the same time in the completion, the full-ness of our joy, insofar as persons are contributory to that joy, we will know and recognize them, happy in their own unique presence in heaven. Should anyone not be a part of heaven, we can be assured that their absence will be covered over by the great bounty of God's love made manifest to us.

Secondly we may have a concern for other beings, those who might live other than "earthly" lives. We are not now referring to an-gels for they have a special existence that is real and not mythical. They are in the faith-cycle of our promised eternity. No, we mean the possible other forms of life which, in the infinite abundance of crea-tion, may inhabit other planets, other worlds or planetary systems. Reasonably, it does not seem that we can deny their existence. In this universe created by an infinite Being, it would seem unlikely that among the myriads upon myriads of stars, and the uncounted created beings that there would not be others who are "similar to" human creatures. Such a conjecture we can reasonably suppose by our obser-vance of the number and variety of creatures which in past, present, and future surround our earthly existence.

But granting this, we also must be assured that these creatures, of whatever form or nature, are not exactly like human beings. This we know because they cannot be, as we are, made in the likeness or "image of God." Why? Because duplication is a limitation of the creative act. Likewise they would not eventually become partakers of our heaven, which is prepared singularly for us, the people of promise. They would not become sharers because of any religious reason, but primarily and essentially because they do not correspond in any way with the revealed salvation which we enjoy. They would not be "born to be resurrected" into eternal life as we were. Why? Be-cause in our faith-cycle only we humans enjoy this salvation promised to us and won for us. God could not, remembering the law of contradictions, duplicate His creation since this would be a weak-ness and not reasonable for the Creator of infinite variety.

To carry this a trifle further, and it can only be a trifle, we can speculate as to the role that created beings of other planets might play in our picturization of heaven. This brings us smack-dab into the very reason God would have for creating other beings. Initially we realize that an infinite variety is evident on earth. Millions of people exist, each one essentially different from every other one, even down to fingerprints and cellular structure. There is in other observed phenomena of nature, such as flowers, insects, etc., an infinite, unending, on-going variety each essentially different.

We come to the question of why this infinite variety exists on earth and why it may extend to existence in further variations elsewhere in the firmament. And the only reasonable answer is found in the basic reason or purpose of all creation — the Creator creates only for His own glory, all must redound to His praise by the very nature of the divine creative act. God must create that which gives Him glory. We can see this reflected in any creative effort even among humans, in their struggles to be singular in what they produce in art, music, literature, or whatever. The Creator acts only for His glory since there is no other to whom ultimate glory such as His can be given.

Also, we can speculate concerning what might be the end or reward of other possible creatures. Perhaps their reward would be in experiencing their own evolution, a progression of one species into many varieties without having to endure death or dissolution. Or, it might be a constant ongoing development toward a perfectibility which they can only anticipate and never really enjoy because it is always coming into being, always expanding into the infinite. Likewise, not having been programmed to die, they cannot seek their own eternal reward since they were not created for a purposeful end as were human beings.

Clear and complete knowledge of these elusive truths will be a great part of our reward in heaven. For we will come to know God as He is in the fullness of His being, and in this knowledge we will have an understanding of all that God has prepared and continues to prepare for His own glory — because this glory exists in God as a fountain which ever overflows to manifest His goodness.

In no way will our own faith suffer when we accept the promised eternal reward. It is a reward of faith — the end of hope in fulfillment. It is the true confirmation of faith which becomes the eternal aspect of the reward. In reason we now see this as both the resurrection of the body and the fulfillment of love. It is ours in accord with God's promise as we understand it, and the love of God is a fire which imbues us by making us one with the very fire, the very Love itself.

In science fiction, in many writings of imagination, mankind has endeavored to describe relationships with other than human created beings, some fellowship which might be shared by living creatures. However, is it not strange that in every imagined representation creatures from outer space are always ill-formed and ugly? Even the robots are not attractive. Do we need this to bolster our egos? Have you ever noticed too that nearly all of these creatures are supposed to be a menace, a "threat" to us? We instill fear by so thinking instead of being eager for friendship. Why should such creatures be inimical to us, why should they be thought of as being somehow superior, stronger and always unfriendly? True they may be of a *different* intelligence but it is doubtful that it would be a higher form because in our faith-cycle we are each created in the image of God in our being and in our soul, and intelligence is the faculty of the soul, par excellence.

In our thinking we cannot situate heaven in any "place" such as a planet or stellar system because each of these has other purpose and necessity in the universe, and in the creative act of God fulfilling His glory. Also, we could not be transferred to another stellar system because we were not created for this, which is for us both a consolation and the goal of our hope as we move toward the fulfillment of our own creation. We were born, we can truly say, for higher, better, eternal things.

Thus, if somehow we were to find ourselves eternally the inhabitants of another planet or located in another cyclic form of life, it would be contrary to the promise given us and therefore unthinkable. We were created for a special, individualized end, and to be rewarded with only another cycle, another trial in time, would be a contradiction of our faith in all that we have been promised. We could not reasonably be rewarded in such a manner that our promised gain would be altered or changed in degree in any whimsical way. Our Creator is constant — more, He is faithful beyond our furthest reach of thought and expectation.

Also, we would not be or could not receive a duplicate of another being's reward, nor a lesser, or second-best reward. Nor would any other created being be rewarded as human beings are to be rewarded. Because, as we know, duplication is a weakness — and also because what is promised to humans as theirs alone could not be shared because it would thereby be diluted or diminished.

All of this merely gives us a final assurance that what we hold by faith, strive for by the devoted and consecrated effort of our lives, will be ours alone. It will be ours as the created heirs that God has called us to be. It will be ours by Redemption. It will be ours by the singularity of our relationship to our Creator. And it will be ours because it cannot be divided or shared with any other beings outside of the promise. This is our reasoned faith, by which we live in hope.

When we think of heaven we do so with the consciousness that it is ours as a right because of the promise and in the light of our fulfilling the conditions of that promise. Thus in our faith-cycle there is no possible alteration of objective or goal. We can say with certainty that heaven for us will be free of doubts and uncertainties, free of the possibility of incurring the wrath or menace of other creatures, and we will be free of their possible envy. The reason for their creation cannot reasonably be identified with our own, nor will our reward be identified in any manner with what their purpose and existence might be. In our uniqueness we have also our hope and assurance in faith.

By this we do not mean to say that other creatures may not know of their Creator and be aware of their own purpose in having been created. Their revelation may be quite apart from ours, indeed it must be, for we have been granted the knowledge of truth to the degree that we can partake of it and follow it to our promised conclusion.

Speculate as we may we cannot change what we possess in faith, nor would we wish to. Other created beings may have been granted a quite different covenant by God, one about which they learn in a progressive manner outside of time as we know it. It has been said that we humans have to be taught about hell, but our real learning in life is about heaven, the pathway to it, and our eventual presence there. Heaven is the place of one's transformed existence after death.

Possession of heaven is our objective and there is no measure by which we can assess what will be ours, let alone make a guess of what may be possible for other creatures. No matter how we come to think about heaven, it is there like the unsolicited song of the skylark, the unstructured beauty of love. When that day of possession comes, and come it must, that our sky is emptied of stars, our sun is black, and no cooling wind is felt moving across our brow, it seems, as we have seen in reason and faith, that somewhere all good hearts will meet and greet other good hearts and all will be merry together. It is heaven where our dreams of unbroken love, freedom from hatred, and our many unanswered sighs will be filled with contentment. It is there that love truly becomes visible and joy is not a reckoning of the sequence of happenings, but it is the one happening itself. "It has been called paradise. It has been called the Tavern at the End of the World," wrote Myles Connally. But it is infinitely more — it is yours — for no vagueness will shroud your end or your reward. Whatever term you may give to this event and existence, you will know it as yours alone. Think upon this with joy.

X

Joy, joy for ever — my task is done —
The gates are passed, and heaven is won!
— Thomas Moore

We have examined heaven quite thoroughly in our limited way. We
have found that we know more than we suspected, but there remains
an infinitude beyond our experience and our present intelligence. It
seems quite an achievement to have revealed for ourselves so much
of what we did not know we knew. This alone should strengthen and
clarify our picture, our understanding of it. At times it is necessary to
do some brooding about what awaits us — we might call it an exercise in using our "intelligent ignorance" which Charles Kettering
found to be a source of genuine hope for those of us who wish to
make progress toward our goal.

The joys and glories of heaven which will for now remain incon-
ceivable still are known sufficiently in revealed truth and solemn
thought to motivate us to seek heaven and all that it promises. As an
inducement we have hope, the great virtue of our longing; we share a
deep desire for the fulfillment of ourselves in everlasting joy. Yet it
remains our own individual choice — we can, just out of natural,
foolhardy perverseness, pass it by.

What Christian, or even well-meaning pagan, would flaunt his or
her ignorance in the face of truth. We have, each one of us, been
given the great, undisputed value, of being created, of being placed
on earth for a sublime purpose. We have been redeemed, made acceptable for heaven because of the infinite merits of God's Son. And
with this we go onward to what is ours by the promise and goodness
of God Himself.

We know that the gift of life itself is a great inducement, an encouraging force for hope. We have all experienced the lavish goodness of the Creator's bounty in bestowing love upon us — this we

cannot deny for, like St. John, we can declare: "From his fullness we have all received, grace in place of grace..." (Jn. 1:16). And each one has felt as St. Augustine: "I strayed in my pride, driven hither and thither by every wind. But all the while it was thy hand which guided me in the deepest secrecy" (*Confessions*). Our hope is in the mercy and love of God. We know the measure of God's love. Our way is the way of prayer and love returned.

With familiar assurance of God's love we can all reach out in earnest pursuit, becoming through our actions His again in the life eternal. We know: "As I live, says the Lord GOD, I have no pleasure in the death of the wicked, but that the wicked turn from his way and live; turn back, turn back from your evil ways; for why will you die, O house of Israel? And you, son of man, say to your people, The righteousness of the righteous shall not deliver him when he transgresses; and as for the wickedness of the wicked, he shall not fall by it when he turns from his wickedness; and the righteous shall not be able to live by his righteousness when he sins. Though I say to the righteous that he shall surely live, yet if he trusts in his righteousness and commits iniquity, none of his righteous deeds shall be remembered; but in the iniquity that he has committed he shall die. Again, though I say to the wicked, 'You shall surely die,' yet if he turns from his sin and does what is lawful and right, if the wicked restores the pledge, gives back what he has taken by robbery and walks in the statutes of life, committing no iniquity; he shall not die. None of the sins that he has committed shall be remembered against him; he has done what is lawful and right, he shall surely live" (Ez. 33:11-16 — Revised Standard Version, Thomas Nelson & Sons, Ltd.).

We know our consolation and possess the instrument to forge our way to love eternal. Again with St. Augustine we can say: "Our salvation is still founded on hope. We do not yet possess it in reality, but God who has given his promise is faithful; he does not deceive you. Only do not separate yourself from him but await the fulfillment of his promise, for eternal truth cannot lead into error. Only do not compromise yourself by failing to carry out in deed what you have with your lips proposed to do. Be true to him and he will hold his promise too; but if you are not faithful, then it is not he who has deceived you but you who have deceived yourself" (*In ep, Joann*, ch. 2). Thomas a Kempis affirms our persistence in seeking eternal love:

"When a certain one often wavered anxiously between fear and hope and once overwhelmed with grief knelt prostrate in prayer in the church before the altar, he thought of these things, saying: 'If I did but know that I should still persevere!' And immediately he heard within himself the divine response: 'And if you did know this what would you wish to do? Do now what you would then wish and you shall be very safe.' And being at once consoled and comforted, he committed himself to the divine will and his anxious wavering ceased" (Bk. 1, ch. 25).

All too seldom do people speak about heaven. They shy away from the subject of hope because they feel themselves inadequate to formulate any clear idea, so they harm themselves by forming none. Perhaps they really fear that too many people are going to be disappointed and should be spared this trouble in anticipation. But who could be disappointed in heaven? Surely not those who have some idea of what the joy will be or what is prepared for them. If there's to be any disappointment it won't be in heaven, and if there is even a remote possibility of your being disappointed you won't be there.

It seems I can hear the voices of those who clutch heaven to their breasts as their special secret. Those who feel they and they alone have themselves "locked in" to a guidance system to get them there easily. Others are shocked to hear anyone speak casually of heaven, or treat it with seeming levity. This book was not written with levity. We have simply tried to take a straightforward look at the place, a look at the destination instead of at the road and its pitfalls and potholes.

For some people, the Bible gives no sure description. They want it spelled out in more scientific terms, or spoken of "liltingly on the tongue" and with a built-in guarantee. When the Bible says that good men shall shine as the sun and shall run about like sparkles of fire among reeds, they respond, "So what!" When you tell the carnal-minded people of today about the things that are of the Spirit of God and hint of what those pleasures may be, the response will be that they really don't care to have their flesh shine or to be like a spark of fire skipping about. Tell someone that the body will be impassable, feeling no pain or harm, no hunger or thirst and the response may be that he would miss being hungry and thirsty. Tell them that they will

103

no more have to live together as man and woman nor turn their thoughts to the carnal acts of generation, and that all voluptuousness will be done away with and you will get the reply that they would rather have things the way they are. And we say this is the compounding of ignorance, or as Lombroso said, "The ignorant man always adores what he cannot understand."

This book considered all that and nevertheless went open-eyed into the night of our small vision. It was not intended to persuade, to crack a whip, or to slap anyone's wrist. Let others do the convincing, put on the persuasive pressure if they will, and according to their lights fit their own extensions onto Jacob's ladder. Our little look at heaven was meant only to sharpen our anticipation, heighten our expectation. It's a mild way of doing your hoping now while you have the time. Those readers who want to enter the undiscovered country will, at least to some degree, learn something of what they may expect. We have only touched on what is known or reasonable about heaven. It goes no further than facts and some rather happy speculation in the light of those facts. A glimpse of glory never hurt anyone — and who knows, it may be everlastingly encouraging. After all, we are here on earth as pilgrims, dewdrops on the morning flower of life.

This undiscovered country may be much as Isaiah declared:

> "The desert and the parched land will exult;
> the steppe will rejoice and bloom.
> They will bloom with abundant flowers,
> and rejoice with joyful song.
> The glory of Lebanon will be given to them,
> the splendor of Carmel and Sharon;
> They will see the glory of the LORD,
> the splendor of our God.
> Strengthen the hands that are feeble,
> make firm the knees that are weak,
> Say to those whose hearts are frightened:
> Be strong, fear not!
> Here is your God, he comes with vindication:
> With divine recompense he comes to save you.
> Then will the eyes of the blind be opened,

the ears of the deaf be cleared;
Then will the lame leap like a stag,
then the tongue of the dumb will sing.
Streams will burst forth in the desert,
and rivers in the steppe.
The burning sands will become pools,
and the thirsty ground, springs of water;
The abode where jackals lurk
will be a marsh for the reed and papyrus.
A highway will be there,
called the holy way;
No one unclean may pass over it,
nor fools go astray on it.
No lion will be there,
nor beast of prey go up to be met upon it.
It is for those with a journey to make,
and on it the redeemed will walk.
Those whom the LORD has ransomed will return
and enter Zion singing, crowned with everlasting joy;
They will meet with joy and gladness,
sorrow and mourning will flee'' (Is. 35:1-10).